'*Vital Flows* is a remarkable book. It takes the reader on an intimate, transformative journey to the heart of psychoanalysis. Through a deeply thoughtful integration of his personal, clinical, academic, and institutional experience, Bolognini presents the evolution and essence of a psychoanalytic identity. The interiority of the analyst as both "rooted" and "winged" interacts with that of the patient to create conditions for an oscillation between fusional contact and protected distance and the discovery and elaboration of intra- and interpsychic experience. The book portrays the simultaneity of the "here and now," "there and then," "everywhere and every time" that characterizes unconscious human experience.'
        Harriet L. Wolfe, *President, International Psychoanalytical Association, Clinical Professor of Psychiatry and Behavioral Sciences at the University of California*

'This is a book of stunning complexity and breadth, a much-needed integration of psychoanalytic theory and technique from a compassionate, master clinician, and story-teller.'
        Fred Busch, *author of* Creating a Psychoanalytic Mind *and* The Analyst's Reveries

'*Vital Flows* is an original, powerful, and emotionally moving masterwork of contemporary psychoanalysis as the multifaceted, deeply human, intra- and inter-connected "science of a possible pathway to the Unconscious." It is a must read for the most seasoned analyst as much as for the beginner, and anybody in between.'
        Eva D. Papiasvili, *Chair, IPA* Inter-Regional Encyclopedic Dictionary of Psychoanalysis

Vital Flows Between the Self and Non-Self

Vital Flows explores the concept of the Interpsychic, or that which exists in our unconscious or preconscious inter- and intra-human exchanges, and demonstrates its significance for understanding psychoanalytic theory and practice.

Drawing on rich clinical material, Bolognini explains how interactions between the self and the ego may be affected by preconscious associations, and how these can hinder the development of our self-concept and social interaction. Combining his international theoretical and clinical knowledge, Bolognini provides meaningful ways to understand the unconscious and renders patients' preconscious channels viable and liveable in a transformative way. With the understanding that the psychic life consists of internal and external interactions equivalent to those that occur by bodily exchange, this text provides an insightful account of how internal life can shape our development from childhood onwards.

As an instructive and topical text, which draws meaningfully from Italian, British, and North-American psychoanalysis, *Vital Flows* will be critical for psychoanalysts and psychotherapists alike, as they seek to understand and apply the inter-psychic within their own practice.

Stefano Bolognini is a Psychiatrist, a Training and Supervising Analyst, and the former President of the Italian Psychoanalytic Society. He is also the former President of the International Psychoanalytic Association, and the Founder and the former Chair of the IPA Inter-Regional Psychoanalytic Dictionary of Psychoanalysis. He is the author of more than 250 papers and several books published in many languages, and lives and works in Bologna, Italy.

THE NEW LIBRARY OF PSYCHOANALYSIS
General Editor: Alessandra Lemma

The New Library of Psychoanalysis was launched in 1987 in association with the Institute of Psychoanalysis, London. It took over from the International Psychoanalytical Library which published many of the early translations of the works of Freud and the writings of most of the leading British and Continental psychoanalysts.

The purpose of the New Library of Psychoanalysis is to facilitate a greater and more widespread appreciation of psychoanalysis and to provide a forum for increasing mutual understanding between psychoanalysts and those working in other disciplines such as the social sciences, medicine, philosophy, history, linguistics, literature, and the arts. It aims to represent different trends both in British psychoanalysis and in psychoanalysis generally. The New Library of Psychoanalysis is well placed to make available to the English-speaking world psychoanalytic writings from other European countries and to increase the interchange of ideas between British and American psychoanalysts. Through the *Teaching Series*, the New Library of Psychoanalysis now also publishes books that provide comprehensive, yet accessible, overviews of selected subject areas aimed at those studying psychoanalysis and related fields such as the social sciences, philosophy, literature, and the arts.

The Institute, together with the British Psychoanalytical Society, runs a low-fee psychoanalytic clinic, organizes lectures and scientific events concerned with psychoanalysis and publishes the *International Journal of Psychoanalysis*. It runs a training course in psychoanalysis which leads to membership of the International Psychoanalytical Association – the body which preserves internationally agreed standards of training, of professional entry, and of professional ethics and practice for psychoanalysis as initiated and developed by Sigmund Freud. Distinguished members of the Institute have included Michael Balint, Wilfred Bion, Ronald Fairbairn, Anna Freud, Ernest Jones, Melanie Klein, John Rickman, and Donald Winnicott.

Previous general editors have included David Tuckett, who played a very active role in the establishment of the New Library. He was followed as general editor by Elizabeth Bott Spillius, who was in turn followed by Susan Budd and then by Dana Birksted-Breen.

Current members of the Advisory Board include Giovanna Di Ceglie, Liz Allison, Anne Patterson, Josh Cohen, and Daniel Pick.

Previous members of the Advisory Board include Christopher Bollas, Ronald Britton, Catalina Bronstein, Donald Campbell, Rosemary Davies, Sara Flanders, Stephen Grosz, John Keene, Eglé Laufer, Alessandra Lemma, Juliet Mitchell, Michael Parsons, Rosine Jozef Perelberg, Richard Rusbridger, Mary Target, and David Taylor.

A full list of all the titles in the New Library of Psychoanalysis main series is available at https://www.routledge.com/The-New-Library-of-Psychoanalysis/book-series/SE0239

For titles in the New Library of Psychoanalysis 'Teaching' and 'Beyond the Couch' subseries, please visit the Routledge website.

Vital Flows Between the Self and Non-Self

The Interpsychic

Stefano Bolognini
Translated by Laura Botherway

LONDON AND NEW YORK

Cover image credit: © Getty Images

First published 2022
by Routledge
2 Park Square, Milton Park, Abingdon, Oxon OX14 4RN

and by Routledge
605 Third Avenue, New York, NY 10158

Routledge is an imprint of the Taylor & Francis Group, an informa business

© 2022 Stefano Bolognini

© 2019 Raffaello Cortina Editore

The right of Stefano Bolognini to be identified as author of this work has been asserted in accordance with sections 77 and 78 of the Copyright, Designs and Patents Act 1988.

All rights reserved. No part of this book may be reprinted or reproduced or utilised in any form or by any electronic, mechanical, or other means, now known or hereafter invented, including photocopying and recording, or in any information storage or retrieval system, without permission in writing from the publishers.

Trademark notice: Product or corporate names may be trademarks or registered trademarks, and are used only for identification and explanation without intent to infringe.

British Library Cataloguing-in-Publication Data
A catalogue record for this book is available from the British Library

Library of Congress Cataloging-in-Publication Data
Names: Bolognini, Stefano, author. | Botherway, Laura, translator.
Title: Vital flows between the self and non-self: the interpsychic / Stefano Bolognini; translated by Laura Botherway.
Other titles: Flussi vitali tra sé e non-sé. English
Description: Milton Park, Abingdon, Oxon; New York, NY: Routledge, 2022. | Includes bibliographical references and index. |
Identifiers: LCCN 2021045433 (print) | LCCN 2021045434 (ebook) | ISBN 9781032132990 (hardcover) | ISBN 9781032132976 (paperback) | ISBN 9781003228578 (ebook)
Subjects: LCSH: Psychoanalysis. | Self psychology.
Classification: LCC BF173 .B634813 2022 (print) | LCC BF173 (ebook) | DDC 150.19/5—dc23
LC record available at https://lccn.loc.gov/2021045433
LC ebook record available at https://lccn.loc.gov/2021045434

ISBN: 9781032132990 (hbk)
ISBN: 9781032132976 (pbk)
ISBN: 9781003228578 (ebk)

DOI: 10.4324/9781003228578

Typeset in Bembo Std
by KnowledgeWorks Global Ltd.

For Paola

Contents

	Foreword	xiii
	Acknowledgements	xxvi
1	Secret passages towards the unconscious: Emotional residences, styles of contact, and exploration	1
2	In spite of my ego: The unconscious and "problem-solving"	15
3	Representation and syntonization: A first taste of the consulting room, between conscious, preconscious, and unconscious: Antonia's first session	37
4	Intimacy and its interpsychic equivalents	45
5	Interpersonal, intersubjective, interpsychic, and transpsychic	59
6	Six commonly used minimal technical tools	74
7	Before the intersubjective: "Presubjective" and "preanalytic" patients in the clinic	83
8	Psychoanalysis and psychosis: Rediscovering the self to rebuild the ego	91

9 "Ubique et semper": Equivalences and consubstantiality between past, present, feared future, and potential future in the analytic experience 119

    Bibliography 145
    Index 154

Foreword

Some years have passed since the publication of Secret Passages and the debate that Bolognini proposes today in this new book picks up from there, from that nucleus of psychoanalytic thought which had introduced us to a peculiar way of doing psychoanalysis and of being psychoanalysts and, at the same time, guided us to an observation point facing outwards to the world.

Bolognini's new endeavour, Vital Flows between the Self and Non-Self. The Interpsychic, starts out from where the author left us waiting for him. Tolerance for waiting is not only an analytical virtue but also an experience that runs through our lives. The reader now encounters a familiar thought, which has continued to "work" on the themes that specifically characterize it and which, over time, has been expanded, deepened and enriched.

The book opens with the image – and it will not be the only one to accompany the reader in the broad framework of the text – of the "walled-up door" in the cellars of his old family home in the Bolognese Apennine hills. The "walled-up door" marks an ideal boundary, separating from "a beyond" that we can only picture through dreams, fantasies, and imaginings, as the author himself did, first as a child then as an adolescent. The image is an effective metaphor that Bolognini uses to introduce us to the "underground world" of analytical work, to the exploration of the unconscious contents we access using "neither hammer nor chisel," and respecting, when appropriate, also the boundary that the "walled-up door" defines.

Foreword

For Bolognini, psychoanalysis is "the science of the possible pathways to the Unconscious." This affirmation, which excludes every kind of idealization and absolutization, immediately gives us the author's characteristic posture and restores a secular view of our discipline, which rejects any temptation towards ideological doggedness.

The epigraph to Chapter 1, taken from a Chinese proverb ("There are two lasting things we can hope to give our children: one is roots, the other is wings"), captures the deep meaning and the specific style of Bolognini's research. The "roots" sink deep into the space of the "old river-stone family house," a space that expands and extends into the well-known and emotionally invested landscape of his homeland, Emilia, and his city, Bologna. Through private references, Bolognini tells us of other "roots," those concerning the bond with family and with the psychoanalytic culture of origin, which nourishes the growth of each and every one of us and forms the "base camp" of our emotional and intellectual stability. It is these bonds that allow us to take flight, feeling sufficiently supported and not too fearful. The more robust our sense of analytic identity is, the wider our range of flight will be, allowing us to explore unfamiliar territories beyond our usual reference points. Bolognini gives us an example of this in Chapter 2 when, addressing the phenomenon of "intuition," he turns to the contribution of cognitive psychology, to something that – as he writes – goes "beyond the specifically theoretical and clinical field of psychoanalysis." We thus have a "taste" of the polyphonic structure of the text, which links the different themes through a multi-voice choir. The specifically psychoanalytic discourse runs alongside references to other disciplines, also literary ones, and historical episodes, memories, and images from the private life of the author, who moves from one plane to another with great assurance.

The "wings," then, allow us to exit the "defensive bastion" in which we risk locking ourselves up and the intertwining of the two terms (roots and wings) produces a fertile growth and a productive expansion both on a professional and personal level. The point is not generic and refers to a theme dear to Bolognini, that of the danger for analysts of falling into a rigid "subjective approach" and an identifying "fixedness" which, as happens in the legal institution of the "closed farm," another powerful image used in Secret Passages, implies confinement within a hereditary repetition (that of the firstborn male son) and the expulsion of everything that appears to threaten that logic. I'll come back to this later.

Foreword

The writing benefits from a simple, almost conversational style, but this does not mean it is simplistic. This is only an apparent simplicity, one that hides – like a tailored suit – a long, patient and painstaking effort, entirely invisible to the naked eye, which creates the elegance of the artefact. Pulling open the folds of this work and "undoing" the intricate weaving that gave rise to the final result is not simple. The book uncoils like a spiral, the threads intertwining, the topic we are reading about shifts from the foreground to the background to make room for another theme, only to reappear later and reclaim its place on the scene, perhaps through another point of view or other associative chains. With the Zen Master Bolognini mentions in Chapter 1, I would say that the book "presents itself," its contents are never assertively declared, and it is up to the readers to be surprised and to listen to its echo or its effects within themselves.

The text holds together some lines of research that reflect the main orientations along which Italian psychoanalysis has developed, both in terms of the analytic relationship and the relationship between psychoanalysis and psychiatry, and in terms of the investigations around the early stages of development. This shows how much the author's theoretical-clinical elaboration is part of a wide environment, in which Bolognini is an active presence both for his contribution in forming it, and for how he was formed by it. On the themes taken into consideration, the author proposes an original point of view, which conveys to the reader the essence of his personal journey. In short, I would describe this essence as a special attention to "psychic exchanges" and to the conditions under which they occur, both at a vertical level between Ego and Self or between different aspects of the Self, and at a horizontal level in the encounter between two internal worlds, between Self and Non-Self, as much in the analyst-patient relationship as in the early stages of development with primary objects. This line of research, which runs through the whole book, is expressed as the central musical theme. It represents the particular attention given to the object of investigation through which the author reads and interprets a vast spectrum of situations, interrogating himself as to how and under what conditions an authentic "interpsychic exchange" can occur, on what gradual steps have to be taken to reach it, and on what this means for the internal structure of the patient and for the relationship.

From this corpus various paths branch out, continuing the author's reflection on his main areas of interest. One of these concerns the concept of the Preconscious, a privileged border area, the "middle realm," which allows the derivatives of the Unconscious to be approached, and within which it is possible to come into contact more fluidly with the states of the Self of the patient and help him become familiar with the Non-Self. This is a central concept in the framework of Bolognini's work, which brings us closer to his idea of psychoanalysis – "the science of the possible pathways to the Unconscious" – precisely because of its quality of being "contactable and experimentable," accessible to conscience without excessive energy expenditure. Green (1974) defines the Preconscious as "an agency that binds," a "tertiary process," which plays an important role of mediation and encounter between the primary and secondary processes, a transitional space between Ego and Id, in which fruitful exchanges between patient and analyst can occur. The practicability of the Preconscious, which Bolognini compares to the system of underground walkways and tunnels that connected castles in medieval times, has many advantages. Transits within this area "allow the customs of the defensive Ego and the Super-ego to be bypassed without duties, controls or disputes" and allow us to work with what is closest to the patient's Ego.

The medieval metaphor is used precisely to indicate the "secret passages", the pathways invisible on the outside along which our internal objects travel and through which we can approach the unconscious derivatives they have managed to filter, making them progressively "mentalizable" and thus helping the patient to "become familiar [...] with his own psycho-emotional life". The author describes an analytical framework that aims to "work closely on what is most accessible to the analysand in the clinical moment, rather than what is least accessible" (Busch, 2014, p. 49). The same rule of directing the interpretation to what is closest to the Ego means respecting what the patient at that moment in the treatment is able to comprehend (take in) and integrate, helping him to proceed from the superficial to the profound, and sparing him the "narcissistic wounds" inflicted by an analytical pretension to access the Unconscious directly, which instead risks fomenting excessive resistance (Green, 1974). The space given to the Preconscious is combined with the author's attention to "reality", "the whole reality" of the patient, not only to "what is behind" – as Semi wrote in the preface to Psychoanalytic Empathy (2002) – and it will be just such a work that will allow us better access to what we affirm to be unconscious.

We find an example of this attention to the areas accessible to the patient in Chapter 6 "Six commonly used minimal technical tools", which looks at some tools often used in dialogue with the patient, which go largely unnoticed and unremarked. The importance that Bolognini gives them derives from the fact that, being "perceived as essentially and consensually natural in the analytic dialogue", they are proposed as useful interpsychic tools that "favour the passages between Self and Non-Self". I will mention just a couple by way of example. The request for clarification, addressed to the patient with a simple "that is?" (in Italian "cioè?"), contains a very rich subtext and serves an important therapeutic function: above all it shows an analyst who is not omnipotent, who can accept his not knowing without shame, an analyst who asks for the patient's collaboration and help, who is capable of revealing his own ignorance or incomprehension. Just as the use of "we" can facilitate or enhance a "good fusionality", where there was none, and cement a working alliance through the "physiological alternation between the sense of individuality and otherness". What emerges is the image of an analyst who has come to terms with his own omnipotent traits and a psychoanalysis at the service of the patient rather than the other way around, as can still happen. To this list of tools, let me add a couple that seem to go in the same direction. The first is being able to admit we made a mistake when this happens and can happen (the search for deeper meanings of what happened will come later), not only to reveal how far removed we are from the idea of being infallible, but also to show our tolerance for making mistakes. The second is being able to express to some extent also the passages that led us to give a certain interpretation or intervene in a certain way. This is a regime of "equal opportunities" in which the patient is granted access, albeit only momentarily, to our internal functioning and the chance to benefit from it in an identification process.

The discourse on the Preconscious introduces the reader to some concepts that are intrinsic to Bolognini's reflections and characterize his work, such as the concepts of Ego and Self. Chapter 2 deals with and describes situations in which the capacity of the damaged Ego impedes "enriching intrapsychic consultations" while at the same time describing the ways in which it is possible to build a fruitful collaboration between Ego and Self in the individual. Bolognini's attention to the demands of the Ego and its functions goes back to the years of his writings on empathy (2002), in which we find a chapter of exemplary clarity dedicated to "analysis with the Ego and analysis with the Self". From those pages we learned how his attention to the Ego was inspired by the definition proposed by Laplanche and Pontalis (1967; Ego as a nucleus of consciousness and bundle of mental functions, as a defensive instance, as a mediating instance between external reality, Id and Super-ego), and how the first acceptation was taken into consideration in the complex tripartite division. Today, in the current text, the discourse has moved on and become more fluid. I thought of some final observations that Laplanche and Pontalis (1967) dedicate to the concept, when they ask themselves whether it is ultimately no longer useful to conceive it as "an internal formation that finds its origin in certain privileged perceptions, which come not from the outside world in general but from the interhuman world" (p. 266). It seems to me that Bolognini's proposition today goes in this direction, affirming that the Ego reflects the complex process of care that we were the object of during our childhood, it is its heir, or, as Bollas (1989) says, it represents "a form of deep constitutive memory".

The focus is therefore above all on the functions that the "Central Ego" of the patient and the analyst perform with respect to the internal objects and the subject's Self, on the relationships between the two terms in the psychic and personal balance. We can imagine a sort of alliance between Ego and Self in which moments of reflective observation (Ego) alternate with moments in which the experiential complexity of the Self prevails. One of the purposes that Bolognini entrusts to analysis is precisely that of helping the patient to create "a cooperative harmonization between the various parts of the Self" and, when these natural synergies or "forms of cooperation" are lacking or have been insufficient in the developmental process, it will be up to the analysis to recreate a good Ego-Self collaboration, repair the flaws and the rigidity, and reopen communication channels that have been interrupted.

The author turns to some conceptual formulae which – as he himself writes – are "dear" to him and which the reader recognizes as specific to and characteristic of his conjecture. The central theme is that of the intrapsychic and the interpsychic, already proposed in Secret Passages, which is enriched and expanded further here also through an elaborate reflection on intimacy. Chapter 5 of the book is dedicated precisely to the interpsychic, in its difference from

Foreword

the intersubjective and the interpersonal. This represents the heart of Bolognini's theoretical proposition and forms a common thread running through the volume: "The fundamental theme is the quality of the individual's experience when he comes into intimate and meaningful contact with the other". The quality of the experience of the current encounter within the analytic couple gives us information about the different modes of encounter that once characterized the mother-child or parent-child couple and provides us with indications about the intimacy and significance of the primary relationships. The interpsychic is directly linked to the "exchanges of internal contents between two people" and their psychic equivalents, to how the internal world of one is combined with the internal world of the other and to the methods of mediation and negotiation, in analysis as in life, between the perception of the Self and the Non-Self, and to the passages (also temporal ones) required for the inclusion of the Non-Self in the Self. The concept of transitionality also contributes to this description, a concept which Bolognini associates with the idea of "intersubjective common/condominium spaces" and which calls to mind those preliminary contacts between psychic, non-intrusive apparatuses, in which – to use the same image – we stay out in the hallway, we do not use first names, and we have not been invited in yet for coffee.

The psychic and relational equivalents of intercorporeal processes – the topic of mucous membranes and their meaning was dealt with extensively in a chapter of Secret Passages – are the tools that bring us closer to the re-enactment of the fundamental "unconscious scene" and inform us about how things went or should have gone in the primary relationship and in the early parent-child exchanges. "Analysts" writes Bolognini "are required to understand the incessant deep flow of symbolic equivalence between corporeality and psychism, adjusting accordingly their daily intimate exchange" with their patients, recognizing their needs (when the inner child is hungry or has stomach ache) and responding to them "as they can and when they can." In the interesting case of Antonia, as in the rest of the clinical material that accompanies the whole theoretical discourse, we can see the intersection of the various planes at work and, above all, observe the intrapsychic relationship of the Self as an object, which reflects the original primary relationships. The analytic relationship offers a new scenario for the interpsychic, one that cannot always be used from the very beginning, while the analyst's listening and observation are aimed at recording as much the quality of the individual's experience when he comes into contact, as the extent to which all this happens. In fact, the author underlines how the interpsychic represents a "wide band" functioning, in which separateness from the object alternates with moments of fusionality, to then recover a fruitful distancing. I emphasize this point, which seems very important to me also from a technical point of view. With patients who did not benefit at the time from a "commensal and cooperative fusionality," our interventions and our interpretations can and must support moments of healthy fusionality, as a way of feeling together with the other, while at the same time helping to build adequate internal tools for facing feelings of emptiness and unbearable loneliness.

"Intimacy," which has its antecedent in moments of special contact and exchange, including inter-corporeal ones, within the mother-child relationship, represents the medium in which a "physiological" communication between two internal worlds is achieved. The discourse on intimacy from the primary relationship expands to reflections around the analyst's and patient's way of being in a session, around the quality of the fluid and creative contact that we are able to create both in the vertical dimension of our psychic space and in the horizontal dimension of the relationship. In the book, a specific paragraph is dedicated to the "working together" of patient and analyst in a "common associative context" characterized by unconscious passages that connect patient and analyst "through a fusional process and a primary identification." The reconstitution or constitution, when this is lacking, of a "functional We," of the "physiological alternation between the sense of individuality and otherness" represent an objective of our work.

The Ego-Self/Non-Self relationship is also found in two other chapters, in Chapter 7, dedicated to "pre-subjective and pre-analytical patients," and in Chapter 8, which deals instead with the relationship between psychoanalysis and psychosis. In this last chapter, the author allows himself a self-disclosure by revealing his ideal theoretical references: the Freud of Mourning and Melancholia, Winnicott, and Bollas remembered for his initial work The Shadow of the Object. They are the authors who paved the way for looking at the Ego-Self relationship "as a condensed intrapsychic functional equivalent of the primary mother-child relationship" and the relationship with the Self as an object, a complex relationship that expresses unconscious fantasies and "the maternal care system" (Bollas, 1989). The way in which the patient treats himself, a reflection of the ways in which he has been treated, is recorded and etched in the intrapsychic and played out in interpersonal exchanges. However, the scope of references and citations of authors with whom Bolognini maintains a fertile dialogue is much broader and never predictable. What shines through in all this is his attention and curiosity towards psychoanalytic thought in its various expressions, the experience and knowledge gleaned from his senior roles in psychoanalytic institutions and from his exchanges with psychoanalysis across the world.

Coming back to the chapters I mentioned before (Chapters 7 and 8), attention is turned to those patients who have undergone very disturbed and inadequate primary relationships, to cases where "nature as a whole becomes an enemy" and what prevails is a veritable "sensory and emotional famine." Before reactivating nutrient exchanges – and this is often possible only at the level of "placental nutrition" – we need to be willing to cross deserts, arid, and lifeless territories, to be where the patient summons us and to "try and try together." In working with severe patients and in post-traumatic situations, Bolognini recovers the sense of the work done at the Ego level – work that can be informative and descriptive, like "looking at a topographic map together" to figure out where you are. A map that forms the basis for a "reduction of energy expenditure" that nourishes the defences, to gain space for the repressed (or, in more serious cases, the split and dissociated) Self, to create a harmony, which may never have existed before, between Ego and Self.

On the economic aspects of the Ego-Self relationship and energy expenditure, it will not be easy for the reader to forget the evocative image of the neurotic patient as someone who does not lose capital (he travels with his full luggage load), but who has to "sustain very high expenses in order to continue repressing," while other types of patient, impoverished by splits and important projections of parts of the Self, travel without baggage, but with considerable losses in terms of capital. The latter are the patients Bolognini categorizes as "Before the intersubjective" (the idea of an analytical patient that has to be "built"), who challenge psychoanalysis by posing a paradox: their problem in fact concerns the poverty of the internal world and the various ways of interacting with it, exactly what psychoanalysis bases its work on. Their apparently adequate functioning on a social level often hides a sterile inner life, an inability to relate deeply to the other, the absence of an exchange from within to within. These are the situations we encounter more and more frequently in our consulting rooms and of which Bolognini gives us some brilliant examples, the case of Renata in particular, but also that of Letizia. The clinical description that accompanies the theoretical reflection puts the reader in contact with the analyst in the field, with the long preparatory work of interpsychic exchanges, with the careful dosage of nourishing moments for the Self and moderate and controlled oscillations with the Non-Self, required for the construction of a "psychic space" and an intersubjective and interpersonal area. In these cases, the experience of otherness must also be wisely tamed before it can effectively become a hub for useful exchange.

I cannot close without mentioning what, in my opinion, is the underlying theme running through the whole book (even if it is never dealt with directly): the analytical identity of the psychoanalyst. Like the musical "phrase" of the Proustian Swann that returns and "rises above the waves of sound," the theme advances on us, surprises us, conquers us, and ingrains itself within us. Bolognini's book is truly the "manifesto" of the psychoanalytic identity of its author. It is a plan that flows on an underlying but continuous level and that emerges through seemingly casual considerations, brief parentheses, and random insertions, revealing instead a precise and personal idea of psychoanalysis, of being and training psychoanalysts, of practising and transmitting psychoanalysis. It is – in my opinion – the deepest and most precious message that Bolognini communicates to us through his endeavour. As readers we are left with the feeling that the author has welcomed us and allowed us to pass through his long analytical experience, both professional and institutional, putting us deeply in touch with the idea of psychoanalysis and psychoanalyst that has evolved within him. I would call it a "secular" and "minimalist" vision of psychoanalysis. I use the latter term to indicate an attitude towards clinical work, as well as towards theoretical elaboration, which is never absolutizing, aware of the multifaceted complexity of our discipline, our limits and boundaries, and very respectful toward those of the patient. As far as "secularism" is concerned, I think of the important pages that Bolognini (2018) wrote about the relationship and the transference movements that every analyst entertains with his chosen theories and with his reference authors. I would like to mention only one point, which specifically concerns a danger inherent in our training: that, when it occurs, of an "excessively strong projective identification of the analyst with a specific inspiring author". If, on the one hand, this absolves us from conflicts and uncertainties, thus producing an obvious and undeniable "economic advantage," on the other, it causes a serious impoverishment, a real "patrimonial damage." The danger of closures and strong idealizations exposes us to the risk of losing our personal identity elements and the creativity linked to the recognition of the transference movements that move our theoretical choices and their elaboration within us.

The temptation to cultivate within ourselves an ideal and highly invested place – whether it be a theory, an author or the very idea of psychoanalysis and the psychoanalytic institution – and to inhabit a hortus conclusus is ever present in our community. The need to relate to an ideal object, besides reassuring us and giving us a deluded sense of protection, can represent the other side of the coin, a narcissistic satisfaction, which counterbalances the harsher aspects of austerity, sensory deprivation and discipline our work subjects us to. However, it contains an insidious danger, that of hemming us into an endogamic and self-referential dimension, which reproduces itself through the generations and which tends to exclude external and diversified relations and creative confrontation with otherness both on a cultural and institutional level.

The image of psychoanalysis that Bolognini leaves us with, also through the clinical narrative which I have not dwelt on but which is an important part of the text, is instead complex, multifaceted, and human. Above all, it pushes towards integration, as he himself affirms in the final chapter of the book dedicated to time. And referring to this dimension, he observes that "the relationship of psychoanalysts with time [...] is also changing in an integrative sense, not only conceptually but functionally, as a technical competence." The ability to oscillate and "dolly" – a cinematic term dear to the author – back and forth between a synchronic and a diachronic position is the mark of an accomplished attitude achieved by psychoanalysis, which having passed through "extremist" phases can now look at itself with maturity and balance. Above all, it can strive towards an integration of the various temporal dimensions that arise in the session: the here and now, the there and then, the everywhere and every time, listening closely to what is relevant at that moment for the patient and in the clinical material.

After leading the reader by the hand through an interpretation of the mechanism of repetition, differentiating it from what recurs and from what is rediscovered, Bolognini takes his leave by presenting us with "the conceptual area of consubstantiality." From a temporal point of view, the idea of consubstantiality expresses the experience of "natural continuity" of the different temporal dimensions that we reach in the session, up to the a-temporal dream dimension, within which the patient's discourse unfolds. "Put simply, I mean that over time and with practice, it becomes quite natural not only to theorize, but to genuinely feel, imagine, think, and portray oneself so that there cannot be great discontinuity between what the patient feels toward external objects, toward the analyst-object, toward some aspects of his remote basic-object, and what he will go on to feel toward future interlocutors of a certain type, as in the past, as now here, as now outside here, as every time that….". The concept of consubstantiality is not limited to this dimension, however, referring to a mode of psychic functioning which represents for the analyst a "resource" and which allows him that "widening of sense […] of what is heard and experienced in the session," as Olympia's clinical case shows us in such an enlightening way.

Discontinuity and change, all possible transformations, will depend, in fact, on who embraces them and how the "every time", what is repeated and what returns is embraced. In the same way, the psychoanalytic object in its fundamental and recurrent structure has been embraced, in the book, by creative thought, and has been returned to the reader revisited, expanded and different.

Paola Marion

Bibliography

Bollas, C. (1989), *L'ombra dell'oggetto. Psicoanalisi del conosciuto non pensato.* Tr. it. Raffaello Cortina, Milano 2018.

Bolognini, S. (2002), *L'empatia psicoanalitica.* Bollati Boringhieri, Torino.

Bolognini, S. (2018), "Incanti e disincanti nella formazione e nell'uso delle teorie psicoanalitiche sulla realtà psichica." In *Rivista di Psicoanalisi*, 3, pp. 533–548.

Busch, F. (2014), *Creare una mente psicoanalitica*. Tr. it. Armando, Roma 2016.

Green, A. (1974), "Surface analysis, deep analysis. The role of the preconscious in psychoanalytical technique." In *International Review of Psychoanalysis*, 1, pp. 415–423.

Laplanche, J., Pontalis, J.-B. (1967), *Enciclopedia della psicoanalisi*. Tr. it. Laterza, Bari 1981.

Semi, A.A. (2002), "Prefazione." In *L'empatia psicoanalitica*, edited by Bolognini, S., Bollati Boringhieri, Torino.

Acknowledgements

I would like to thank *Rivista di Psicoanalisi, International Journal of Psychoanalysis, Psychoanalytic Quarterly, Psychoanalytic Inquiry, Journal of the American Psychoanalytic Association, Revista Peruana de Psicoanálisis, International Forum of Psychoanalysis, Revue Française de Psychanalyse, Le Coq Heron, Forum der Psychoanalyse, Psicoterapia Psicoanalitica, Docta, Revue Psychosomatique, Revista de Psicoanálisis de la Asociación Psicoanalítica de Madrid,* and *Psychotherapies* for permission to publish papers (partially revised here) which had previously been presented in their annals.

I am also grateful to the editor Routledge/Karnac for their permission to publish revised excerpts from "In spite of my Ego. Problem solving and the Unconscious" (in *On Freud's "The Unconscious"*, edited by Mary Kay O'Neill and Salman Akhtar, "Contemporary Freud series," Karnac, London 2013) and "In between sameness and otherness. The analyst's words in interpsychic dialogue" (*in Donald W. Winnicott and the History of the Present: Understanding the Man and His Work*, edited by Angela Joyce, Karnac, London 2015, pp. 17–30).

My gratitude is also due to the editor FrancoAngeli for permission to use part of the material related to the chapter on "The relationship as an analytic function" (in *La relazione psicoanalitica. Contributi clinici e teorici*, edited by Nicolino Rossi and Irene Ruggiero, Milano 2017).

I am profoundly indebted to Paola Golinelli for the constant exchange of theoretical and clinical reflections we have shared over the years.

A special thank you, finally, to all those colleagues in Italy and across the world who have so generously contributed to the evolution of the thoughts contained in these papers, through their discussions at various congresses.

1

SECRET PASSAGES TOWARDS THE UNCONSCIOUS

Emotional residences, styles of contact, and exploration

> There are only two lasting things we can hope to give our children: one is roots, and the other is wings.
>
> Chinese Proverb

Over many years of analytical work, I have had the opportunity to observe how for many people the tangible place where they live bears no relation whatsoever to their deep emotional residence. Many live in a different city or country, having moved away from their places and families of origin at a young age for all sorts of reasons to do with external reality (most commonly study and work) and/or internal reality (e.g. the need to distance themselves from family relationships with too much or too little involvement).

What has always struck me, however, is the persistence, albeit not always entirely conscious, of powerful underground ties with those places and with those families. Ties which are often minimized or subjectively denied, but which endure to the bitter end constituting authentic *invisible symbioses* (a term that we owe to the investigative creativity of José Bleger, 1967). Ties which reveal themselves in all their dramatic strength at critical moments, such as the loss of a parent or the disappearance of elements of the *fantasmatic base camp* we carry inside ourselves, deep down, even though we are geographically distant and seemingly oblivious.

I have always been struck (even if this is not the most edifying of examples, it renders the idea) by those stories of big city mafia clans in 1930s and 1940s America who, when faced with key decisions, clung with almost religious devotion to their family roots, often in remote villages deep in the Sicilian hinterland. Those places where powerful bosses from Brooklyn or Chicago regressed to their origins by consulting the "families", thus revealing emotional residences and internal scenarios that were surprisingly different from their actual geographical locations.

Cinema has provided us with unforgettable representations of these individual and group intrapsychic geographies.

Nowadays, an interesting indicator of individual scenographic backdrops is given by the choice of start-up screen picture on our computers. Whether they show faraway and exotic ideal places, or – as is most often the case – everyday environments and people that are familiar to us and that are part of our present or past existence, these images reveal basic scenarios that form the backdrop to our internal lives; and we place there, ideally and not always consciously, many of the fantasmatic movements that contribute to making us what we are and how we feel.

Each of us has our own scenario, then, an internal scenario in which our own lives are more easily represented, either concretely or symbolically by analogy. Just like everyone else, I too have my scenario, which I will present now to give you an imaginable (but not overly or exclusively abstract) setting for some psychoanalytical thoughts.

The old river-stone house in the Bolognese Apennine hills, cradle of my childhood and the backdrop to so much oneiric life for me and my relatives, has a small door on the ground floor. This little medieval door, carved out of solid walnut, stands opposite the staircase to the upper floors and leads down to the cellars. Until the end of the 1950s, it was a hive of comings and goings down there. I remember it very well: men busy unloading heavy cases from carts laden with grapes, for days on end, exchanging only a few brisk business-like words; women sitting on the ground clipping the grapes and boxing them up for market, chitchatting in dialect; the smell of the must in the vats, the large silent barrels and thousands of bottles all in a row; tastings, business, and bargaining; we children watching and listening, eagerly taking it all in. The cases of grapes were transported on farm carts pulled by oxen, as tractors, and cars were still few and far between. It was a peasant world not so dissimilar from that of the 1700s and 1800s, when you think about it, with all the associated social injustices and with a variegated unfolding of sounds, colours, and human interactions that are unthinkable today.

Today that world is gone. All those people are gone, however, impossible that seems to me. "Absence, presence more intense", wrote Attilio Bertolucci (1929), and that's the truth. The house is still there, but no one lives there anymore. Today, stepping through that little walnut door, you are cloaked in heavy, velvety darkness, enveloped by the dense mystery of the centuries and absorbed in their silence.

Going down the steps, by candlelight, you come to a cobbled hallway, filled with barrels and vats that have lain empty for decades, from which other mysterious doors fan out.

One of them is walled up.

A little further on, an even smaller door of very dark, timeworn chestnut wood is the main attraction for the now rare visitors: it leads into the very heart of the cellars, a network of narrow tunnels carved into the rock in days gone by, which led to the icebox (where winter snow was stored for the pantry) and to a long narrow tunnel stretching to the base of the hill, once an escape route in case of enemy invasions.

The outwardly peaceful and unremarkable Bolognese Apennines hide a surprising subsoil riddled with twisting turning medieval transit routes dug by hand with spade and pickaxe. A sort of rabbit warren in which each secret passage had its own dramatic *raison d'être* and its own more or less adventurous history connected with those dark centuries.

But, truth be told, it is that walled-up door that has always held the intrigue for me: especially since I realized that the floorboards directly above it (on the ground floor), make a hollow sound when you knock on them.

What lay beyond that door?

From that hollow sound I deduced that there had to be something, and from the fact that such an intricate and imposing door, with its ancient brick arch and river-stone masonry, would not have been justified without a room of some importance behind it.

Why had they walled it up, presumably a few centuries ago judging by the type of masonry?

Secret passages towards unconscious

I knew of other walled-up rooms under those house and other similar houses in the area, uncovered during renovation work: but in those cases, the spaces had been filled with waste materials, pottery shards, old wood, other stones etc. Not here: it echoed empty.

As a child, I postponed to adulthood the possibility of knocking down that wall and seeing what lay beyond that door. As a teenager, though, I did hazard a couple of attempts on my own initiative, with a hammer and chisel. But before I could remove a single stone, the house elders stopped me, I don't remember why.

Then I went to university, out into the world, and my interests shifted away from that cellar. I didn't give it another thought; until, in analysis, the walled-up door reappeared in dreams with inescapable force, taking me by surprise.

In one dream, a turning point for me, I finally entered the large room that had been closed off for so long: and what I discovered (or, rather, rediscovered) there changed my life.

An interesting detail in that dream, when I think about it today, was that I did not have to use hammer or chisel to enter that secluded place and discover its contents. Please keep this detail in mind.

In his famous book *Zen and archery* (1948), the German philosopher Eugen Herrigel, having moved to Japan for a few years to teach Western philosophies, decides, in turn, to immerse himself in the local culture. It takes him a long time to understand that no mechanical or intentional technique is needed to draw the bow and shoot the arrow.

The Japanese Master could not explain it to him in philosophical terms, effectively, if he hoped to produce a real transformation in him.

All he could do was sit by and guide him through that experience as best he could, with a sort of weary patience. Until the moment he snapped awake, excited, as Herrigel, by then exhausted and exasperated after months of slogging away in unsuccessful attempts to draw the bow, suddenly fired off a shot, almost by mistake.

The Master jumped to his feet, bowed, and declared, with solemn approval: "Today *it* shot!".

Professor Herrigel, who for months had secretly been trying to outwit him with various techniques to draw that confounded bow, was caught off guard by some part of himself that had pre-empted him, escaping the control of his conscious intention. What had happened? Again, difficult to explain.

Secret passages towards unconscious

In any case, the Master explained that he had not bowed *to him*, but *to the event*: "it" had shot.

In psychoanalysis, there is almost never an effectively voluntary and programmable *Open Sesame!* moment of access to the Unconscious, nor is there anything magical about our work.

What there is, instead, more often than not, is a long, patient and analytically painstaking psychic cohabitation that can produce openings and transformations, awaiting something that will come, if it comes; sometimes through *krysis*, but more often through slow and laborious *lysis*.

This underlying disposition is what marks out a psychoanalyst: few people know how to tolerate the breadth and tension of silence, of waiting, of saying nothing if for the moment there is nothing to say, even before knowing how to interpret (from the Latin: *inter-pretium-dare* = to give a price, a value, a sense to) anything.

Strange as it may seem, few people are able to bear not knowing, and all too often even analysts feel the need to believe they know what is going to happen, what is coming, what is on the other side of the wall of that mysterious cellar; what the Unconscious is made up of, what is inside it, how to open it, how to enter inside it, what can be understood about it, and what (if anything) can be done with it.

Our theoretical and clinical research is without a doubt useful and necessary, and by now hundreds, if not thousands, of colleagues are worthily dedicated to it, following the currents and fronts that suit them best.

Yet the reality of our daily practice means that most of the time we start out with only a very faint idea of where we will end up with each patient, and paradoxically it is precisely this uncertainty that lends wisdom and dignity to our science and our profession. For this reason, if a patient in consultation asks me how long the analysis will last, I can reply with steadfast serenity that it is not a question of determining how long the analysis will last, but how long *his* analysis will last. I might even point out to him that if someone were to hazard a prediction (worse still, with an air of smug arrogance), that someone would certainly not be a psychoanalyst.

Sometimes, when this sort of request is presented to me with a particularly aloof and superior attitude, I am tempted to respond just as condescendingly with a famous phrase coined by the American baseball champion Jogi Berra, a quipster who drove reporters crazy: "it's tough to make predictions, particularly about the future".

Our strength lies, rather, in the method, together with the experiential trust built up over many generations of analysts, ourselves included, who have been helped by psychoanalysis above all – let's be clear – in our personal lives.

It is true, however, that those secret passages leading to the Unconscious do exist, and perhaps they await us – in the sense that there is an ambivalent, conflicting but very powerful desire for internal contact in every human being. And every so often we all uncover some of those secret passages, either our own or those of others.

Our specific expertise, tempered through years of practice and exchanges with colleagues, usually keeps us from backing away and wasting the opportunity of exploring those secret passages; which is no small thing.

Almost 120 years after the publication of Sigmund Freud's *Interpretation of Dreams* – the date the birth of psychoanalysis is conventionally traced back to – we are constantly improving our knowledge of the complex physiology of the analytical process and the many configurations and developments that can manifest themselves within it. And yet we have no means of predicting their sequence, alternation, intensity, and duration, because each analysis is its own unique story.

We discover many secret passages together with our patients. Establishing who unearthed them first is perhaps not so important.

At some point, the Zen Master would say, *it shot*, and this *event* is what matters.

The preconscious

The truly significant fact is that these potential passages are available within us in a primarily conflicted way, and they are a source of great surprise to us when we happen upon them and make use of them.

Much has been written about the Preconscious, and I have found the most fruitful contributions on the subject in Lopez (1976, 1983), Green (1974), Filippini and Ponsi (1992), and Busch (2014).

But much still remains to be written about this area – even if it may appear dated due to its strong roots in the context of the first Freudian topic – as in the session it can prove incredibly fertile. Within it, we dolly back and forth between primary process and secondary process, between rationality, memories and more or less nonsensical fantasies, in a fluctuating dimension very close to the oneiric. The apparent vagueness (or so it appears to the layperson…) of our reliance on associations and complex perceptions is redeemed by the rigorousness of the setting that we take care to maintain, and by the articulated internal structure with which we give space and credit to the Preconscious itself.

Over time we come to trust ourselves enough without overestimating ourselves or our official status as "psychoanalysts"; and that is when we are able to be psychoanalysts for real and not just on paper, floating without too many expectations or pretensions, in a sufficiently calm and potentially creative suspension.

Resigned, nevertheless, to not knowing anything in advance, and to the fact that we do not become "psychoanalysts" once and for all on being handed our ministerial diploma, but day by day, session after session, if this contact is kept alive with ourselves, with our patients, with our colleagues and with the significant objects in our personal and scientific lives.

Different depths: Identifications with authors

Of the many metaphors for investigating the Unconscious at its various levels, the classic ones relate to exploring the sea depths, which can be used to evaluate – without overly idealizing – its real cognitive possibilities. Here is one that may well irritate those who place an overly exclusive, abstract and idealizing value on the so-called *knowledge* of the Unconscious.

On 26 January 1960, the famous Swiss underwater explorer Jacques Piccard succeeded in diving, in his bathyscaphe, to the dizzying depth of 10,916 metres in the Mariana Trench (Pacific Ocean). The bathyscaphe was built to withstand the tremendous pressure of the water, and Piccard and his assistant Walsh, protected by its steel casing and with the aid of powerful headlights, were able to see through a thick porthole that even at that depth there was life: on the seabed they were amazed to spot some strange types of sole and shrimps, bleached of colour and ghostly looking.

The experience of those two deep sea explorers, albeit very important, was essentially visual; had they come into direct contact with that environment, they would have been crushed by the pressure, blinded by the darkness and frozen by the temperature of the water.

Like the Nautilus in *Twenty Thousand Leagues under the Sea*, the depths, the truly fathomless abysses, were visited and illuminated from within the safe confines of a totally protective, strong, metal container, capable of withstanding pressures, temperatures, and disorientations that no human being could survive.

In the same way, the deep Unconscious is viewed through a porthole: the psychic equivalent of a thick glass plate separates the explorer from the surrounding environment and protects him.

Knowledge acquired in this way is *theoretical*, in the etymological sense of the term (i.e. visual, from the Greek *theoréin* = to see), and this is the only way in which the Mariana Trench – both the real one and the symbolic one – can be explored and known.

Likewise, analysts who are able to glimpse into the depths of the patient's Unconscious are for the most part incapable of really entering into contact with it or treating it directly. Through the porthole of their analytical vision they can, at best, begin to get their bearings and cautiously start the shared process of bringing deep materials closer to the Preconscious, which will be the psychic level of maximum interpsychic treatability in analysis.

Here, psychoanalytic technique shows two distinct and fundamental areas of competence:

- *how to foster the process of representation*, passing from the "Mariana Trench" of the true Unconscious to the contactable, experimentable, shareable, and progressively mentalizable Preconscious, which can be symbolized by the modest but not insignificant depths accessible to a normal swimmer, floating freely with no protective capsule;
- *how to familiarize the patient with his psycho-emotional life with a certain continuity*, so that the experiences do not manifest themselves through symptoms, acts or pre-representational magmatic somatizations, dissociated from the rest of the Self, but instead become an integral part of the subject's full experience.

In popular imagination, the illusion that *seeing/understanding in the abstract* magically produces transformation and healing, touches one of its highest illusory peaks in the patient's initial expectations regarding the therapeutic process: "the analyst will interpret, explain, I will understand and I will instantly change!" As all the experts know, that's not the way things work.

Analysis can be extraordinarily effective, but almost never in an easy, rapid, explanatory, and hetero-induced way. What is actually needed in many cases is a substantial and painstaking shared work, which is far more complex than most people imagine, but very familiar to analysts, both in theory and in their daily practice.

This is the only way the Mariana Trench can be explored and known, and the mythical dreamlike submarine drawn by little Richard during a session with Klein (1961) can roam the great depths using interpretations that may well be brilliant in their reconstruction and visual description of an objective underwater world, but that are mostly deductive and in many cases incapable of directly involving his Self.

No child could wander about experientially and naturally in those abysses, and neither could his mother or his father, or his analyst.

And yet, theoretical knowledge, in light of our *Working Ego* (Fliess, 1942; Schafer, 1983) in the *analysis with the Ego* (Bolognini, 2002), is also extremely important: it guides us along the path, allows us to give things a name and a meaning and suggests to us otherwise inconceivable representations, even when it does not allow us to have a live, direct and full contact with them.

Psychoanalytic theory is a scientific (and in many cases hypothetical) expression that is nevertheless valuable and necessary for the working Ego; the *working Self* (*Ibidem*), with its experiential and sensorial content, is the area of the analyst that should participate and harmonize with this more active, descriptive and investigative ego component.

I would add that the metaphor of the submarine (which allows visibility in otherwise unliveable conditions, preserving the subject's Self from a more complete, momentarily unsustainable experiential contact) may in some cases also contain a warning about the analyst's potentially excessive projective identification with a specific inspiring author: from *inside there*, that is, from *an insulating and impermeable state of identification with one or more authors/submarine* who have formulated strong psychoanalytic concepts, it is possible to see clearly (to *theorize*) with the utmost effectiveness and speed, and the analyst can feel protected by being contained in an armed, and sometimes even armoured, theoretical apparatus.

The risk, which is often overlooked, however, lies precisely in that possible loss of contact with one's own Self which is intrinsic to states of excessive projective identification towards an object that is *internalized* ("taken inside") but *not introjected* ("not digested").

Becoming the other a little is a healthy process, which can be used as an echo sounder when it is temporary, partial and at least to some extent manageable, as in *trial identifications* (Schafer, 1959, 1964, 1983). But it can degenerate dangerously into solid, structured and unwitting forms of true identification: when, in simple terms, one *becomes* the other, but loses oneself.

Of course, there is an immediate economic advantage in those solid identifications with the author, in that we travel faster and seemingly unburdened of our conflicts and our uncertainties (including theoretical ones). We have *become* the other, the admired author or expert colleague, and – what is more –being no longer ourselves, we have temporarily freed ourselves of many of our limits and tensions. At the same time, however, we must painfully acknowledge a severe "patrimonial" damage to the Self, due to the loss of our authentic identity elements.

In this way, if an analyst works not *with* Freud, Klein, Bion, Winnicott, Kohut, Lacan etc. – as happens if there has been a good introjection that respects separateness – but instead slips into unconsciously *becoming* one of them, he loses himself along the way (Bolognini, 2013a, 2018).

Identification, in its true form, is by definition an unconscious phenomenon (Grinberg & Grinberg, 1976).

Relationships with authors, not unlike those with important figures from our childhood, constitute for each analyst a further place of internal declination of the transference, which we all have to deal with well beyond the end of our analysis.

We have the interminable task of cultivating our relationship with these internal psychoanalytic objects, relating to them intensely and creatively but without allowing them to become substitutes for our Self; admiring and loving them, when their qualities allow us to, talking with them, learning and enriching ourselves with partial introjections, but respecting their otherness.

If we board the submarine forgetful of our fragility, finiteness and real identity, we lose the internal contact and the sense of ourselves.

Some readers may remember a Japanese cartoon from the 1980s in which a boy *became* the mega-robot Goldrake, by entering his head/control cabin, taking over the controls and omnipotently accomplishing great feats: well, that is not the right dimension for us.

We will come back a number of times to this slippery and deceptive point, where the quality of the analyst's training can be severely put to the test, beyond any level of learning or conceptual updating.

Coming back to the more practicable preconscious

Experiential integration is realistically possible, however, in the Preconscious. There, ending up in the water is not a tragedy, since the depths are modest and liveable, even if the inexperienced usually need some preparation and acclimatization, much like in a swimming pool.

The beauty of this acclimatization is realizing that we can float, bob up and down, gradually gain confidence in ourselves and the environment, that we can entrust ourselves to a different fluidity and to a reality that follows unexpected codes a far cry from those we were used to, but that we are not barred from.

If regression works as it should, the person who begins an analytical journey enters into contact not only with his repressed anxieties and frustrations, but also with the wealth of the many parts of himself that have been hitherto excluded in various ways or kept segregated one from the other. The associative river, suitably assisted, dissolves the mortar of the walled-up door, reclaims its stones and the "wall" crumbles a little at a time, with no ruinous collapses and no forced drilling, reopening previously inaccessible areas.

Within those areas, the patient can then encounter figures and internal situations that have been awaiting him for years, and that asked to return to the scene by re-emerging from underground prisons; or to come to light by finally completing an unfinished, uncertain representational gestation and emerging from the limbo of the unrepressed Unconscious.

Regression, if properly assisted, can get the games started again and restore life, oxygen and freedom to the Preconscious, making it a more familiar, more fertile and ultimately liveable area.

Intra- and inter-psychic energy savings

The economic aspect of preconscious psychic life is significant, and you will find extensive considerations on this topic at several points.

The practicability of the Preconscious, when this is possible, allows considerable energy savings usually, because the (more or less secret) passages allow the customs of the defensive Ego and the Superego to be bypassed without duties, controls or disputes.

Fewer delays, less effort and fewer restrictions; thus, the temporary deficiencies in full mentalization can be progressively integrated.

Coming back to the image of the old house in the Apennines, I am reminded of the ingenious early medieval devices used to send voice messages from one floor to another in houses and castles: intramural acoustic pipes forged with *Eustachian horns* and carved into the rock, similar to the conformation of the inner ear, which allowed whoever was in the cellar to speak directly with the upper floors without wasting time and energy. In this way, without having to go back upstairs or shout too loudly, the word made its way from the cellar to the second floor, bypassing the first floor, like a sort of *intercom*.

In a similar way, those ancient inhabitants had wisely fitted the attic granaries with intramural pipes (vertical ones, in this case, running in a straight line) so that wheat and flour could be passed directly down to the ground floor, without people having to trudge down the stairs with a heavy sack on their shoulders.

Rapid messages without a messenger

Let's remain, for the sake of metaphorical continuity and richness, in the historical imagery of the Middle Ages. That dangerous era, in which almost every castle had adequate defences and provisions to withstand lengthy attacks and intrusion attempts (and here we analysts draw immediate analogies with the intra- and inter-personal defensive dimension against traumatic transpsychic break-ins …), but in which sieges were commonplace and made communication with the outside world problematic. How did news and messages get from one place to another?

In peacetime, the classic way and a metaphor for conscious interpersonal communication from Ego to Ego, was that of a messenger, on horseback perhaps, who brought the dispatch with him.

But, in reality, that is not how things worked in many cases, and today we know from historians that news travelled much faster, so that in Rome it was possible to know in a relatively short time what had happened in Milan, Bologna, or Florence.

The network of castles was, in fact, surprisingly interconnected through an articulated system of sounds (bells), smoke signals (daytime), fires (night-time), and reflective mirrors.

Each castle had to be visible to at least one other, and the sound or light messages travelled far faster than a horse: *mirroring castles*, we could say, continuing our metaphorical game where we can imagine an interpsychic that is not necessarily mediated by the Ego, whose defences could interfere heavily at times, perhaps suppressing the messenger (and – with him – the message/connection).

Incidentally, I consider research on mirroring neurons (Rizzolatti & Sinigaglia, 2006; Gallese et al., 2003) extremely interesting for psychoanalysts (see the brilliant interdisciplinary review presented by Falci [2017]), both for the findings themselves and for the perspective and methodological premises adopted by neuroscientists, which are so different but which coincide with ours in many respects.

I believe, however, that we should not lose sight of the fact that they necessarily concern – at least for now – a rather precise and circumscribed level of interhuman empathic situations, whose real complexity very often goes beyond the rather primitive levels of intentional premonition and predictability implicated in those elementary phenomena (Bolognini, 2004). I ascribe to human empathy, and to psychoanalytic empathy more specifically, a much greater depth and cognitive complexity than that described and studied so far, however admirably, by neuroscientists.

Coming back to the medieval metaphor, let us try to imagine not only the mirrors with their rapid and concise ciphered language; not only the messenger on horseback with his dispatch; not only the procession of dignitaries in carriages with their official and emphatic declaration of the message manifesto; but also and above all the most amazing of medieval feats: the network of underground routes that connected the castles to one another, allowing men at arms and sometimes even animals to pass back and forth.

The system of tunnels in Emilia, for example – evidence of which can still be seen today – connected the fortress of Savignano sul Panaro with that of Bazzano and the fortified Abbey of Monteveglio. Legend has it that this system (divided into sections due to the difficulty of aerating the tunnels) allowed Countess Matilde of Canossa (1046-1115), the foremost mediator in the medieval conflict between Empire and Papacy, to pass secretly through there with her dignitaries, escorted by her armed guard.

In other words, switching from medieval metaphor to psychic life, the contact and dialogue with internal objects sometimes travel along pathways invisible on the outside, but can allow entry into even the most inaccessible fortresses. Of course, that requires the basic trust necessary to venture into the visceral depths of the Self.

We do not venture into those depths alone, at least at the beginning.

They are depths that we shared – if things went the way they were supposed to go – first of all with our mother, and with our father too if things went even better; and with others as well if life has been particularly generous towards us. Then, if necessary, analysis reopens the games later in life and outside our close family circle; and assisted and partially shared regression takes us back there, where physiological fusionality (Pallier, 1990; Bolognini, 1997, 2002, 2018; Fonda, 2000, 2019; Bonfiglio, 2018, 2019; Lombardozzi, 2019; Meterangelis, 2019) can be established again, and where an intermediate creative area can reopen between the Self and the Non-Self. This area does not yet fully correspond to the conscious and declared *We*, but within it the internal contents of one (starting from milk, but also its subsequent physical and psychic equivalents) can flow into the other, on the basis of vital desire, pleasure and trust, until introjection in its most authentic and profound form.

At that point, the *Non-Self*, the disturbing and often unacceptable *Other*, can gradually transform itself a little at a time into the other (with a small "o" …), in the sense of another separate and recognizable person. This is how we nourish ourselves, this is how we relate to each other, and this is how we develop and grow.

In genital love, as adults, we will also find this possibility of letting "something internal" flow from one into the other, from within to within, through underground, intimate, mucosal, exclusive relational pathways, capable of getting past even the most hardened defensive fortifications (Bolognini, 2008a) in a natural way.

The interpsychic must be recovered by reopening those pathways, or else it must be rebuilt, or in some cases built from scratch. The pages that follow are dedicated precisely to this dimension which from *inter-* (in the primary relationship) can be introjected and become *intra-*, until it is playable again, as a reference, as *inter-* in adult life as well.

A potential pathway where nothing is guaranteed at the start, but where much can creatively be brought into play, when the vitality and ability of internal relations assist us.

Before entering the experiential terrain of the clinic, however, I ask you to follow me for a few more pages in an exploratory digression on the invaluable function of the Preconscious.

2

IN SPITE OF MY EGO

The unconscious and "problem-solving"

> Those men are few who, because of the fortunate endowment of intuition, are allowed to do something less than a minute analysis of concepts. To them belongs authority, but they cannot be, nor must they be, imitated.[1]
>
> Friedrich Julius Stahl

The topic of energy saving and intra- and inter-psychic fluidity has long inspired in me a series of reflections that go beyond the specifically theoretical and clinical field of psychoanalysis.

In meandering through my associations, influences, and memories, I was struck by the internal perception of an acute feeling of envy in calling to mind some figures that are part of my personal experience. Those figures are characterized somewhat by a strikingly intuitive aptitude and by a seemingly instinctive ability to face up to and resolve a variety of problems.

This envy is well-justified, in my opinion, and strays just beyond the bounds of admiration – a physiological and well-hidden envy about which I feel no shame or guilt. On the contrary, when all is said and done, it even leads me to feel a certain sense of solidarity with myself. How does one *not* envy those persons who seem endowed with the gift of not having to seek out solutions to certain problems, because instead of seeking out those solutions …they find them?!?

I will try to explain.

Some people are said to be *endowed with practical sense*, in the broad definition and not necessarily in reference to concrete or manual abilities (in many cases they might be more accurately described as *pragmatic*). Others are summarily described as *intuitive*. Others are still as capable of instinctively regulating themselves in more complex situations, giving the impression not of puzzling over things in a more or less rational and obsessive way, but of inventing useful solutions with a certain quick and easy creativity.

And if, in many cases, one manages to observe a conscious, well-functioning Central Ego at work in these people – one capable of effectively focusing on the problem, of not losing its way or getting worked up counterproductively in facing the task at hand – in other cases, one observes something more surprising and less comprehensible. That is, certain people actually seem to bypass the normal processes of detection, analysis, and working through of the problem, and instead land smoothly and directly on the solution, goodness knows how.

We can take for granted that in this description of mine there is a certain idealizing emphasis due to the intent to highlight this kind of impression and phenomenon; we can also agree, then, that I may be exaggerating a little in setting aside a special category for this type of mental functioning in the realm of problem-solving. Nevertheless, there seems to be some truth here, in the widespread recognition of the (albeit somewhat rare) phenomenology I have described.

Moreover, it is precisely this feeling of envy that has allowed me to reflect on this topic with greater curiosity and with more motivation, in search of the "secret" of these surprising abilities – to the point where, for all intents and purposes, I consider it the driving force behind the considerations that follow.

In Chapter 6 of *The Unconscious* (1915b), "Communication Between the Two Systems" (p. 74), Freud makes a very important comment on the psychic work carried out by the Unconscious:

> It would nevertheless be wrong to imagine that the *Unconscious* remains at rest while the whole work of the mind is performed by the *Preconscious* – that the *Unconscious* is something finished with, a vestigial organ, a residuum from the process of development. It is wrong also to suppose that communication between the two systems is confined to the act of repression, with the *Preconscious*

casting everything that seems disturbing to it into the abyss of the *Unconscious*. On the contrary, the *Unconscious* is alive and capable of development and maintains a number of other relations with the *Preconscious*, amongst them that of *cooperation* [our italics]. In brief, it must be said that the *Unconscious* is continued into what are known as derivatives, that it is accessible to the impressions of life, that it constantly influences the *Preconscious*, and is even, for its part, subjected to influences from the *Preconscious*.

And later (p. 78):

It is a very remarkable thing that the Unconscious of one human being can react upon that of another, *without passing through the Conscious*. This deserves closer investigation, especially with a view to finding out whether preconscious activity can be excluded as playing a part in it; but, descriptively speaking, the fact is incontestable.

Of these two fascinating Freudian passages, I would highlight, then, two fundamental concepts:

1. the Unconscious, too, *works* (and, as Freud says, it sometimes *collaborates*);
2. the Unconscious can be activated; for example, it can combine with the Unconscious of another, *eluding* the Conscious.

Many authors have explored the work of the Unconscious, focusing mainly on dreamwork, understood differently from classical *oneiric work*, which is destined above all to mask latent content. Almost all the authors I will cite have been fascinated, in fact, by the variability of the combination of the primary process and secondary process that sometimes seems to be created in the dream, produced in a sort of *joint venture* between the Unconscious and the Preconscious, in the absence of the conscious Ego.

It would therefore seem appropriate to differentiate these two activities of the Unconscious, naming the one we are referring to *oneiric working through*.

We will see along the way how this work of the Unconscious in collaboration with the Preconscious can more easily be manifested when there is a certain internal psychic arrangement, which usually involves the subject's conscious Ego being put in *standby mode* or having a very discrete, peripheral and non-invasive presence.

This aspect will be dealt with in the second part of this chapter.

In the first part, I will try to describe some processes that I think maybe fundamental in at least a partial comprehension of the creativity of the Unconscious and its problem-solving capacities.

The unconscious as an area of active transformation

In *Secret Passages* (2008a), I summarized some inspirational contributions of that time that, even though they differ greatly, are all oriented toward the perspective of a *sensible* Unconscious, one that is *at work* in the dream, and potentially transformative:

> Adler (1911) spoke of the dream's *functions of premeditation*; Maeder (1912) spoke of a *function ludique* of the dream, as a preparatory exercise to subsequent operations in external reality; Grinberg et al. (1967), describing *elaborative* dreams in phases of integration, highlighted the patient's growing reparative capacity as he begins to know how to take care of himself; Garma (1970) outlined a *broad way of thinking* during dreams – an archaic-type thinking, intensely visual, but one in which judgments, reflections, criticisms, and other mental processes exist, belonging to the same type as those of being awake; the theoretical line that starts with Winnicott and extends to Bollas placed value on the experiential dimension of the dream; De Moncheaux (1978) hypothesized a reintegrating function of the dream with respect to trauma; and Matte Blanco (1975) re-examined a possible aspect of displacement in dreams, like an opening – at times, a creative one – onto possible new places, times, and representations, and saw condensation as an attempt at integration of different spatiotemporal categories.
>
> There are still others: Kramer (1993) was concerned with the effects of dreamlike activity on the mood-stabilizing function, and Greenberg et al. (1992) with the increase in REM sleep in situations of complex learning. Fosshage (1997) brought out the generally synthetic function of the primary process, which emphasizes, through highly intense sensorial and visual images, the affective colouring of the experience.
>
> (p. 153)

I mention this overview of contributors – who are by no means homogeneous and only partially relevant to the topic under examination – because I consider them to be united, at any rate, by their interest in a mysterious component of working things out that exists at a deep oneiric level: *something, unbeknown to the Ego, works, combines, assembles, conceives, creates, and transforms.*

The history of philosophy and the history of science are rich in famous examples of dreams that opened the way to a solution to the dreamer's extremely difficult problems (just think of Bohr's dream on the composition of the atom). Even ancient literature and mythology make frequent reference to an intense unconscious activity that is the bearer of unexpected solutions capable of taking the subject's conscious Central Ego by surprise.

It is especially in dreams that the gods appear to mortals and tell them what to do in crucial moments: apparently *magical* solutions springing up from deep sources rather than from conscious reasoning by the subject's Ego.

At a less abstract level, I think that the well-known fable "Puss in Boots" beautifully illustrates in metaphorical form what we are considering here.

Puss in boots

The story, of popular origin but narrated in different eras by Giovanni Francesco Straparola (15th Century), and later by Giambattista Basile and Charles Perrault (17th Century), by Ludwig Tieck in 1797, and finally by the Brothers Grimm in the 19th Century, tells of the youngest of three sons of a miller. On his father's death, the only thing the boy inherits from him is a cat, while his brothers receive more substantial bequests.

Left alone with the cat, the boy is anxious because he does not know how to get himself out of unfortunate and apparently impossible situations; his mind is constricted by desperation, and he sees no way out. And that is when the cat (an underrated but extremely intelligent animal, held in high esteem by the boy's father) sets about inventing appropriate solutions!

Having ably engineered an excellent rapport with the king on his master's behalf, making him believe that he is in the service of a noble gentleman, the cat completes his masterpiece by inducing an evil ogre to transform himself into a mouse, thus eliminating him.

In this way the boy will acquire the ogre's castle, and the suitably high social status that goes with it.

What is the cat?

It is an instinctive part of the boy, endowed with an unexpected genius in the area of problem-solving that takes everyone by surprise.

The boy (in turn a metaphor for a potentially valid and promising, but still immature, conscious Central Ego) is too constrained and weighed down by his difficulties, and perhaps also by a basic feeling of inadequacy, to be able to think or to act accordingly.

The cat, by contrast, instinctive and unprejudiced, bypasses any inadequacy anxieties with a healthy dose of omnipotence (after all, he wears "seven-league boots"). He upends the situation, transforming the invincible ogre into an easy to deal with a mouse, and in this way bestowing power (the ogre's castle) on the boy, so that the boy will feel he has the adequate status to be able to marry the princess.

But wait a moment: all praise to the extraordinary cat, yes, but hats off to the boy as well – for not being opposed to these developments, for not feeling diminished by the different roles the two of them played, and for tolerating his own passivity in relation to the cat's initiative. He was not blinded by envy of the cat's intelligence.

In metapsychological terms, the maturing conscious Central Ego (the boy) knew how to recognize and respect the occasional superior creativity of the combined Unconscious/Preconscious (the cat) in these instances, giving it space without narcissistically opposing it and without allowing his desires for control to prevail over what was happening.

All this is by no means a foregone conclusion. We find ourselves observing not a single unexpectedly gifted and capable unit, but instead a *(structural and internal) couple* who collaborate well, thanks to the fact that *one of them lets the other work in areas where the other works better.*

Perhaps something of this sort – here played out on the level of internal objects and parts of the Self – had already happened long ago between the child (then playing the part of the "cat") and a figure who was crucial to his life experience. Had someone allowed the child to explore and to develop areas of competence? Had someone understood favourably – and perhaps with some surprise – a natural, existential talent of his?

As you will already have noted, I am describing a *favourable situation in the internal relationship between an individual's Ego and his Self,* and I am alluding to *interpsychic parental styles* and to originary formative events that, once *introjected*, can then produce just such a positive situation later in life as well. This can truly constitute the most precious of inheritances, just like in the fable.

Fortunate are those who received this at home, at the beginning of their life. We strive to equip our patients and our students (future analysts) in the same way.

We will come back to this point later. For now, I wish to limit myself to hypothesizing about and describing *a potentially and occasionally creative oneiric area, which is based on the possibility of representation, decomposition, and recombination of the elements at play in the subject's internal world, thanks to the reliable and reconnecting effect of the primary process, and to the reorganization permitted by secondary process*, which alternate in varying degrees.

This is how the joint work of the Unconscious and Preconscious proceeds.

The Ego can either go along with it or oppose it. And, in some cases, popular wisdom goes so far as to invent rituals or customs that perform the function of letting the Unconscious and the Preconscious work, putting the Central Ego to rest: as in the example that follows.

The little guatemalan dolls

There is an enchanting Central American custom that seems to me to provide an enlightening metaphorical representation of what I have just outlined in metapsychological terms, and that was described to me many years ago by a patient of mine who had just returned from a trip to Guatemala.

To better contextualize this metaphor, I will start with some clinical background that is not incidental; on the contrary, it is quite consistent with the fact that the patient brought to her session precisely this associative material, and that she engaged in a small case of acting out: she gave me a gift (a concrete one).

The patient had been in analysis for four months and was going through a felicitous and markedly benign regression typical of the *analytic honeymoon*. In my belief, she was reproducing a positive primary experience of fusion and nursing (her traumatic problems had occurred subsequent to that phase).

In a wholly significant gesture, the patient gave me a little treasure: a Guatemalan lucky charm that consisted of a little box with six dolls in it, each one different from the next.

"The popular custom", she explained to me, "is to place the six little dolls on the headboard of your bed in the evening. You recount a different problem to each doll, then turn out the light, and go to sleep. During the night, the six little dolls talk to each other, and in the morning, you have a different view of your problems!"

This custom fascinated me, and – in addition to considering the meaning this story had for the patient – I set about reflecting on the benefits that this custom could bring to those who practised it. For example, it could help them sleep more soundly because their problems have been entrusted *to someone else*. Furthermore, it determines that more than a certain number of problems (in this case, six) cannot be dealt with at any one time, thus setting a limit on a possible flood of anxieties and disturbances, establishing a container.

But, above all, it establishes a basic trust in the existence of an unconscious process of working through and transformation, which takes place in the absence of the conscious Central Ego (while the subject sleeps) and can produce substantial changes in one's vision of things.

With the defensive vigilance of the Ego lowered, the containment of anxieties – recounted and entrusted to *someone/something* else (the dolls) – and the creative recombination of contents (a *solution* in the double etymological meaning of *release* and *resolution*) due to the primary process seem to be happily condensed in this private little ritual. The work will take place in the dreamer *partially unbeknown to the conscious Ego, but with its agreement,* given its acceptance of the ritual.

The overall atmosphere of this scenario is homely, intimate, and on a human scale. Here, the work entrusted to the Unconscious is implicitly understood as a natural resource that can be drawn upon without fear.

Intuition

Let us take a step back, for a moment, and return to the phenomenological aspect of the processes we are exploring.

The concept of *intuition* (from the Latin verb *in-tueor*: "look inside") designates the kind of apparently instant knowledge that does not pass through cognitive reasoning or a sensate process, and that seems, instead, to surge miraculously from deep down.

Intuition has had a very tumultuous development and reception in philosophy, starting with the era of the great thinkers of Ancient Greece, who gave it multiple readings and definitions. In considering intuition, they sometimes focused on sensorial functioning, but more often on that of the intellect, with a strong tendency toward the description of transcendent experiences and the idea of immediate perception of the *first principles* (as in Plato and Aristotle).

My personal impression, in revisiting some of those ancient thought processes through philosophy texts, is that, in general, philosophers intended to place a decidedly high value on intuition, attributing special characteristics and functions to it (often insistently contrasting it with mere sensorial perception), but that these texts do not offer many interesting insights on the nature of the psychic processes involved.

What seems to me to be far more stimulating for the study of this phenomenon, instead, are certain contributions of cognitive psychology, even if they are not so useful for understanding the underlying processes and even if they are generally snubbed and frowned upon by analysts.

In 1926, for example, Graham Wallas studied the processes that lead to creative problem-solving, describing four typical stages:

a. *preparation of the task*, in which one tries to describe and understand the problem in its various aspects;
b. *incubation*, a sort of decanting period in which the subject does not think about the problem and instead focuses on other things;
c. *illumination* (or *insight*), when the solution to the problem is suddenly revealed in an unexpected way (something analogous to the *Aha! Erlebnis* of phenomenologists);
d. *assessment*, when the cognitive Ego lines up with the intuitive parts, providing an integrating explanation of what has been acquired.

An example of this process comes from the testimony of the French mathematician Henri Poincaré, who used to dedicate a couple of weeks to the phase of *preparing the task* and then refrain from it, dedicating himself to other pursuits. He would then go on to reap the sudden and unexpected *burst of illumination*, while he was busy with geological excursions and other studies. This pattern brings to mind analysts' analogous capacity for suspension, which I like to define as their being "happily resigned" – from a certain point on in their professional development – to letting themselves be surprised by the spontaneous and unplanned emergence of interpretive solutions and empathic intuitions (Bolognini, 2002). This can occur for analysts after they have ceased all intentional mental acts of investigation and instead entrusted themselves to fluctuating attention.

Janet Metcalfe and David Wiebe (1987) demonstrated that *problems requiring a creative solution can be effectively resolved quite suddenly*. Their interesting study involved asking researchers who were subjected to a problematic situation, at four-minute intervals, to what degree they felt they were advancing toward a solution to the task. The results showed that an awareness of progress was very much present in processes that involved strategies aimed at reproducing experientially verifiable situations, while it was absent in processes characterized by intuitive *leaps*.

Moreover, already in 1945, Max Wertheimer had hypothesized, from a gestalt point of view, that *creative intuition may emerge when the individual grasps new relationships between elements of a problem*. Edward De Bono (1970) traced this back to the *capacity for lateral thinking*, a special mobility of the observing centre of gravity based on assuming a potential multiplicity of points of view in considering a problem.

Conversely, among the obstacles to these intuitive processes we can find the complex phenomenon described in Psychology as *subjective formulation* (*impostazione soggettiva*, Rumiati, 2006), related to problem-solving patterns that are so repetitive and habitual for the subject that they impede him from considering alternative pathways. This concept calls to mind the idea of *functional fixedness* (Duncker, 1945), which is more connected, however, to the repetitive consideration of objects' characteristics.

Continuing to draw on the field of psychological research, I would like to close by mentioning a very popular concept that has had extremely productive applications across all sorts of spheres: the concept of *brainstorming* (Osborn, 1962), especially interesting when it is connected to a group setting.

If a portion of shared mental work undoubtedly takes the form of a simple expansion of the operational capacity of the various "working Egos" in the group, in other ways, and on other levels it is nonetheless undeniable that brainstorming produces something more than a simple summation of cognitive resources. Perhaps the phenomenon of brainstorming resonates with Freud's (1915b, p. 74) comment quoted at the beginning of this chapter: "it is a very remarkable thing that the *Unconscious* of one human being can react upon that of another, without passing through the *Conscious*".

Here, I think, we are in the realm of the work performed by the six little dolls in the Guatemalan ritual. Only, in brainstorming the individuals are awake and are real people.

And yet there is something similar here. Does it depend on a shared lowering of Ego defences? Is the interpsychic a factor, perhaps?

Connections between cognitive theories and the psychoanalytic view of intuition

As a psychoanalyst, I am inclined to revisit these stimulating contributions from cognitive theory, which in a certain sense predict and describe the 'surprise effect' compared to the subject's habitual viewpoint, and I am minded to integrate them with certain psychoanalytic concepts that seem to me invaluable in shedding light on some aspects of intuition.

I am referring, for example, to functional derivatives of *processes of partial identification* (Grinberg and Grinberg, 1976), which can be produced in a physiological way in the internal world, if there have been *multiple, adequate introjections of useful and positive objects and of their functions*. These internal objects are the stable and structured intrapsychic equivalents, if you will, of the six Guatemalan dolls.

Expressed in other terms, it is easier for the subject to be able to assume multiple points of view – which are different but can nevertheless be well coordinated and adequately condensed – if he has experienced, to the point of stable introjection, a similar way of being in some of the figures who were significant for him, and who are present and accessible in his internal world.

For this process to take place, however, these profound identifications must not be absolute and therefore must not end up substituting the individual's Self. There must be structure and a certain degree of internal separateness in the usual way of functioning.

That is, the subject must be able to "consult" his internal objects, putting himself partially and temporarily in their shoes, but "with a round-trip ticket", so to speak – identifying with the objects and their points of view, but also managing to reclaim his own observing and organizing centre of gravity. In this way, he retains both a sense of self and a good internal mobility toward other objects, *without "fixing" on an identification with any one of them.*

This internal mobility, which is not conscious and not intentional, but which actually unfolds in a natural, syncretic way over a very short time, could perhaps be "laid bare" in these terms: "how would these things be viewed by ... my father? ... my mother? ... my teacher? ... my friend?", etc.

And the plurality of the "consulted" objects could be connected to the integration and cohabitation of more family figures, who enrich the child's reality.

In my language (Bolognini, 2008a), I consider these processes to be *the Central Ego's capacity to consult internal objects*; in this way, the Central Ego can draw on the creativity and richness of these internal sources and on their diverse perspectives.

An even more detailed analysis of the levels of interiorization (a general term used to group together all the processes through which an object is brought from the outside to the inside) requires some basic questions to be clarified:

- *inside* what? Inside the Ego or the individual's Self?
- how far *inside*? And in what way?

Following the criterion of a certain functional equivalence between bodily and psychic processes, we can describe the various degrees and types of interiorization in this way:

- *the object is taken into the mouth,* tasted, controlled (it is not swallowed and it is not spat out, until the subject decides to carry out one of these two actions that would lead to his no longer having control over it), and in this way, some of its characteristics can be known, such as form, consistency, flavour, etc.

    This level (*incorporation*) is at play in *conscious imitation*: the subject can experience some of the object's characteristics and mentally reproduce some aspects in a conscious way, detaching from them, however, without difficulty, and without lasting modifications in the subject's own internal world.

    Professional actors – especially comedians, specialists in caricature – develop a certain degree of psychological mastery and technique in deliberately carrying out these operations when they imitate another person.

- *The object is swallowed, but not digested.* In this way, the object is *taken inside*, occupies an internal space (concretely, in the stomach), and can no longer be voluntarily controlled, except in the intentional vomiting of anorexia; but it remains inside as a whole object and does not become part of the individual's Self (literally, of the organism's cells). It is other than the self, even though it is *inside*.

The object is *internalized*. Processes of *projective identification with the internalized object* are possible (the subject, identifying with it, *becomes* the object), but *at the price of a certain replacement of the Self* with that object.

In general, this situation is pathological. Partial introjective identifications are not accomplished with individual functions (see the following paragraph).

In these cases, the person does not succeed in consulting his internal objects, both because – being in a state of projective identification with one of them – he sees the world and tends to function only according to the perspective of the object with which he is identified, and because, in the absence of any internal separation, he cannot dialogue with any internalized object.

- *The object is digested and goes on to become part of the bodily Self.* The psychic equivalent of this is the acquisition of characteristic partial functions received from the object, which begin to become an authentic part of the subject's Self and Ego through introjection of the nuclear Self (Wisdom, 1967).

We are then in the area of *partial introjective identifications*.

But this tableau also includes the *internal relationship with whole objects* (e.g. the father, the mother, or a teacher) who are well preserved as a memory, a representation, and an affect, with whom to relate without their replacing the subject's Ego with actual identifications.

Hosted within the Self, distinct from the subject's conscious Central Ego, they can become *objects for consultation*.

I maintain that, on this basis (deriving, substantially, from Object Relations Theory), the *specific obstacles to the consultation of internal objects* can be responsible for the phenomenon of *subjective formulation* described by Rumiati, pertaining to repetitive patterns of problem-solving that interfere with the consideration of alternative pathways, as well as Duncker's previously cited concept of *functional fixedness* which is the further consequence.

These psychological concepts effectively describe the dysfunctional result of internal arrangements that impede creative intuition and "fishing" for solutions from the unconscious–preconscious area.

Psychoanalytic Object Relations Theory allows us to portray the internal scenario that makes in-depth consultations either possible or impossible, as well as the alternation of points of view and a certain part of the work of the Unconscious.

To sum up, I hypothesize that, in their rigidity, *subjective formulation* and *functional fixedness* implicitly reveal a clear, excessive bond of identification by the subject with a single object of reference, which has taken the place of the Central Ego (which would generally be more wide-ranging, were it healthy), *to the point of colonizing it.*

This object is not infrequently a parental occupant figure with whom the subject's Ego is projectively identified totally, to the detriment of his own authenticity, spontaneity, and curiosity.

Incidentally, this is precisely the problem of those analysts who have remained too intensely and exclusively identified with their own analyst, or – even more frequently – with their supervisors. These analysts have *become* their objects, who in this way replace their Self, so that they cannot truly consult them.

Deidealizing intuition

The previous paragraphs have been dedicated to the study of the *subjective formulation* and *functional fixedness* from a psychoanalytic point of view.

Now I would like to address another specific aspect of intuition, connected not so much to the problem of the *variety* of points of view as to the *speed*, or lack thereof, of the process.

We owe to Heinz Kohut some interesting, disenchanted, and not at all idealizing comments on the phenomenon of intuition, which can help us progress further. According to Kohut (1971), *the mental processes that appear to be intuitive* and that typically impress the observer, to the point of making him believe he is in the presence of very special powers, different from ordinary ones, *in reality differ only in the speed at which the mental operation is carried out.* That is, the operation has so struck us as to make us assume the presence of extraordinary ways of functioning. In addition, Kohut observes (p. 291):

> Talent, training, and experience will at times combine to produce results, in a variety of areas, which strike us as intuitive; thus, we might find intuition at work not only in the field of complex psychological states (such as is employed by psychoanalysts) but also

[...] in medical diagnosis, or in the strategic decisions of a champion chess player, or in the planning of a physicist's experiments.

This comment about the speed of the process – among other things rather tangential, since Kohut relates it almost incidentally in a chapter otherwise dedicated to empathy – seemed a little reductive to me at first. But with the passage of time, I have re-evaluated it (probably also because it implicitly limited the possibility of idealizing and envying the "magical" resources demonstrated by intuitive subjects ...).

I believe that Kohut may have been onto something here, and that it may be worth exploring the problem from another point of view. For example, if Kahou'ts hypothesis is founded, what could cause that loss of speed in mental functioning?

In other words, what can obstruct, overload, or clog up otherwise naturally rapid and effective thinking processes?

And, to continue our exploration, what useful acquisitions can come to our aid, in this sense, from the comparative study of neurotic pathology and psychotic pathology?

Energy expenditure and Ego functioning

The study of neuroses from an economic point of view has revealed that there is a characteristic **expenditure of energy in repression**: that is, the counterattacks necessary to keep conflict-generating content repressed entail an elevated economic cost, of which general fatigue, convolutedness, and a functional slowing down of thought can at times constitute symptoms accompanying those more specific to neuroses.

In my style of language, *the neurotic travels with his entire* (symptomatic, oneiric and economic) *load as hand luggage*, in a system of increasingly precarious and costly repression into the dynamic Unconscious, and the patrimony of the Self is not detached and projected far away.

Continuing on a metaphorical level, for the most part *neurotics do not lose capital* (the patrimony of the Self is repressed, but not split); *they must, however, sustain very high expenses in order to continue repressing* and maintain within the unconscious "*caveau*" those conflictual elements that would upset the arrangement of the Self's "day zone". Exhausted by the demands on their energy, they have – so to speak – very dark circles under their eyes, extreme fatigue, and indeed neurotic symptoms.

Complication, convolutedness, inhibition, and slowing down of thought processes can be the result of continual, counterproductive interference by internal conflicted components that prevail upon the Ego, limiting its normal working capacity, and of the energy expenditure that saps the Ego's strength.

The slower speed of mental processes would make rapid intuitive moments very rare, according to Kohut's observation.

My additional hypothesis is that, in many cases, the Ego's capacity to give space to the creative contributions of the Preconscious and the Unconscious may also be damaged. In a state of internal alarm and consequent increase of ego control and of functional contracture, the subject does not allow himself to make use of enriching intrapsychic consultations with internal objects, and he does not experience their points of view or their ways of being, getting stuck in the *subjective formulation* described by Rumiati and in Duncker's *functional fixedness*.

In terms of metaphorical equivalents, *the neurotic would then regulate himself intrapsychically in the manner of those persons who, in their defensive mode, "no longer listen to anyone" externally and avoid interpsychic exchange.*

Alternatively, we could describe this dynamic by imagining that the boy in the fable by Perrault and the Brothers Grimm did not welcome the help of Puss in Boots, or that the Guatemalan no longer wanted anything to do with the dolls that worked for him by night. But here we are already moving away from the economic aspect of the energy expenditure that is necessary to repress the creativity of the Unconscious/Preconscious area, an expenditure due to conflict.

Conversely, *patients capable of marked splitting and projections of internal parts of the Self are simplified, impoverished as much in content as in the articulation of the Self, and are consequently "lighter"* (I would say that they "travel without hand luggage"). They are relatively asymptomatic, and, if anything, they tend toward the maniacal.

In economic terms, they *lose "a portion of their capital"* ("capital" intended as patrimony of the internal world, as standard equipment of the Self, and as the abundance of internal object connections), detaching themselves from that capital and forfeiting it in a way, since by doing this they avoid conflict. In colloquial terms, these are the people, for example, who *don't make a fuss*, who *cut to the chase*, and who – like Alexander the Great facing a Gordian knot – do not waste time trying to undo the knot, but instead simply slice through it with a single sword stroke.

In a specific way, *when important splits of the vertical type come into play* (to the point of dissociation, understood in a psychoanalytic and not a phenomenologically psychiatric sense), which have the effect of compartmentalizing experience (Gabbard & Wilkinson, 1994), the mental functions and contents tend to be organized according to a simplified arrangement of personality structure.

In these split states, *the subject travels without hand luggage,* having shed the "weight" of a part of the Self – more or less as a lizard does when, exposed to danger, it drops its tail leaving it for the aggressor so that it can run away faster.

In this compartmentalized, simplified, and impoverished condition within the Self, people are, however, generally asymptomatic, and they experience less stress and fatigue precisely because they avoid, at least in part, the economic waste involved in a conflict, and very often delegate someone else to represent and projectively experience whole parts of the Self.

The picture I have described with regard to the use of splitting/dissociation can fall within frank pathology or – when limited in quantitative terms and confined to a simple tendency – it can at the most characterize a certain personality type, constrained but decisive (and we must not forget that the etymology of the verb *decides* stems from the Latin verb *de-caedere,* "to cut away from").

On the other hand, in the entirely physiological case of *functional specialization of the "Professional Self",* which is compatible with good health, the fact that a person at work is organized in a relatively split/dissociative way can be necessary and even useful. If all surgeons identified with the people they operate on, they would no longer be able to do their job; and if all attorneys were not advocates for their clients but instead retained a constant, fully integrated sense of humanity, they would lose too many legal battles – and so on.

Subjects do specialize, with temporary functional splits for the purposes of the task at hand, and often a white coat, a black gown, or a pair of overalls worn on the job are the equivalent of a *suitably split internal set-up,* assimilated and then consolidated with society's full consensus.

The economic advantage of this internal simplification, through which the person is functionally transformed into a highly specialized character and is focused with intense investment on certain selected functions, *can produce an associative fluidity and speed of mental passages compatible with functional rapidity of an intuitive sort.*

If this optimal reduction of energy expenditure is then combined with a non-conflictual possibility of contact and of internal consultations with significant objects, this generates, in turn, an increased richness in the mobility and variety of points of view, with a true "kaleidoscope effect" in accelerating functional times.

Conclusions on the theme of intuition

I have tried to indicate, with this rapid cinematic dollying between physiology and pathology, some psychic processes that demonstrate the participation of unconscious and preconscious levels in the work of problem-solving.

I have also briefly explored the area of intuition, proposing some hypothetical connections between the phenomenological observation of this area and some aspects of how it might be understood psychoanalytically.

I would like to devote some final, broad reflections to the different perspectives from which the contribution of the Unconscious to problem-solving has been more or less explicitly considered in diverse cultural spheres, before closing with a concise formulation of a possible psychoanalytic vision of this topic.

Very briefly, it could be said that:

- many Eastern cultures seem to converge in considering the subject's conscious, logical and rational Ego as an obstacle to the free expansion of potential internal knowledge. At times they recommend extremely sophisticated methods of gradual deactivation and functional suspension of the Central Ego, through meditative practices, ritual techniques, exercises in abstaining from thought control, diffuse fusionality with the environment, or regression piloted in various ways toward fusional conditions of pre-separation.

    In these cultures, the Central Ego is not generally suppressed, but partially scaled down and placed on *standby*, as a potential impediment.

- Cultures of a psychedelic Western type tend to openly devalue the Central Ego's function and force a suspension of the Ego through its functional suppression, based on the ingestion of substances. Basically, the Ego is intentionally and pharmacologically numbed. These cultures emphasize a presumed sapiential contribution of this pointless deregulated experience, with aspects of a (narcissistically invested) claim for the right to regress omnipotently to an intrauterine, *oceanic*, and pre-separative psychic state, largely at odds with the demands of reality and with the expectations of the rest of the human race.

- Cultures of the arts and crafts traditionally assign a more dignified status to action than to thought. In artisanship, competence in the manual accomplishment of the task is especially valued; in art, the work of art itself is what is valued above all, being strongly invested with narcissistic libido.

  The Central Ego, however, is the project advisor and the auxiliary assistant to the artisan, whose hands are usually the most invested part; the Unconscious of the artisan engaged in working is above all the Procedural Unconscious, the seat of skills and abilities that have become automatic.

  In the artistic field, the ideal aim is to reach a level of *mastery* that relieves the conscious Central Ego of control functions. For example, the great violinist establishes a direct bridge *between heart and hands*, given that his technique is no longer for him a problem to be regulated and monitored by the Central Ego's surveillance.

- Psychoanalysis never intends to eliminate, deactivate, intoxicate, or pharmacologically numb the Central Ego. Since its inception, it has renounced manipulation of the attentional state and thought control through hypnosis, which Freud abandoned very early on. Psychoanalysis is not interested in paralyzing the prison guard (the defensive Ego, when it is such), but in transforming it in its relationship with the other parts of the Self.

  One of the aims of contemporary psychoanalysis is that of permitting a *cooperative harmonization between the various parts of the Self,* repairing and restoring the internal functional synergies that are missing in the pathology.

  Such synergies, by contrast, are established naturally during development, when the child and his relational objects have the opportunity to experience *forms of cooperation* (in sucking, in learning, in interpsychic interchange) *that are then introjected* and gradually structured into a way of functioning that also becomes intrapsychic.

When the developmental and formative process takes place harmoniously, the subject's internal demands cooperate with equal participation in situations of suffering or conflict as well, maintaining an internal sense of cohesion and reducing splits to a minimum.

A benevolent Central Ego – faithful, capacious, and tolerant, heir to the primary objects that have formed its capacities and functional articulations – knows how to intervene when it is useful, and how to step aside when other parts of the Self demonstrate superior creativity and competence suited to the task. The Ego is then called on again, at the end of the process, to provide a central, integrative contribution to what was produced from the contributions of the internal parts. The cohesiveness, atmosphere, style, and fluidity of these internal relationships allow us to perceive the greater or lesser harmony that characterizes various people in their way of living with themselves and with others.

I think that it was precisely the perception of this internal complexity that led Pessoa (1982) to write: "my soul is a hidden orchestra".

From intra- to inter-psychic (and vice versa)

If in the intrapsychic the *secret passages* allow for fluidity, rapidity, and unexpected savings, in the interpsychic they are no less important.

I could probably be accused of having taken the bend too wide and that nowadays excessive references to the Preconscious might sound out of place: an anachronistic insistence on the first topic, in the strict sense, in an age where things have progressed far beyond that from various theoretical and clinical points of view.

Yet, for me, psychoanalysis is not exclusively and abstractly the science *of the Unconscious* (constantly exposed, among other things, to the necessary risk of a shift from investigation to speculation). It is also, and above all, the science *of the possible pathway to the Unconscious* and of the natural relationship (which in fact means episodic, usable, and meaningful) with it. I believe that our work nevertheless requires us to pass *through it* to reach that area in which the Central Ego fishes but of which it is not master. An area in which – if things go well enough – the Object or Objects benevolently assist the Subject in learning from the experience.

In analysis, for the most part, we do not provide the patient with any cognitive-descriptive information about their Unconscious. Instead, we train the person, session after session, to exercise the contact, passage, accessibility of the pathways that can bring them closer to the Unconscious: as Confucius says, we do not give the hungry man a fish, we try to teach him gradually how to fish. And, above all, today, we go *fishing* together with the patient.

I had the good fortune of learning how to fish – in a concrete, not metaphoric, sense – in the bountiful waters of the Venetian rivers of the 1950s and 60s, with one of my father's friends, a skilled fisherman who was patient and thoughtful, and who taught me no end of lessons by direct example. He showed me how to tie hooks, how to choose the right line, floats, and lead sinkers for different types of water (rough or calm, deep or shallow) and for different types of fish, and how to readjust strategically to handle a particularly robust and combative catch – such as a pike – without ripping the tackle to bits.

Last but not least, he provided me with a living example of the ability to wait during those long spells where nothing seemed to be happening, especially when fishing deeper waters, where the potential interlocutors were the larger, cannier fish, wilier and more elusive.

I learned from him and then we each fished on our own, keeping a certain distance so as not to get in each other's way. I will always feel a profound sense of gratitude toward that person, and I consider him to be one of my great masters, included in the list of worthy individuals that naturally includes my analyst and my supervisors, among others.

Remembering these people so clearly, their thoughts and their ways of being, makes me feel as if I could have an internal dialogue with them, and I like to recreate and rediscover this atmosphere of dialogue within the community of my colleagues.

In several studies dedicated to the interface with neuroscience, the prefrontal area is mentioned as the place of rapid connection between the deep emotions of the basal nuclei and the secondary cortical levels. I like to imagine the prefrontal area of analysts as an *agorà*, a marketplace for communications, an area of intense hustle and bustle in the analytic dialogue and in the individual reflection, a transit route for a potentially harmonious connection/composition of human complexity. One day we will know more, but already now we can glimpse the experimental proof of something that is familiar to us in our psychoanalytical clinical work.

Ultimately, we would do well to ask ourselves: the pathways to the Unconscious…yes, but to which Unconscious? …and to whose Unconscious? …to the Unconscious of the patient or that of the others we interact with too?

The answer to these questions does not seem impossible, then.

The pathway to the Unconscious, the contact with our internal world and that of others, the ability to exchange at different depths, are almost never one-directional. The conditions of permeability, practicability, and accessibility of the internal world concern reciprocal realities.

I believe that, all things considered, my father's friend was happy not to go fishing alone and that teaching a pupil the techniques, just as someone else had probably taught him, gave him a sense of satisfaction.

I also believe that if a psychoanalyst can no longer work with his patients, for reasons other than retirement, besides the tangible economic loss there would also be a deep sense of sorrow linked to the interruption of vital functions intrinsic to the (albeit professionally structured) relationship.

Note

1 Translation from an Italian translation of the original German by G. Atkinson.

3

REPRESENTATION AND SYNTONIZATION

A first taste of the consulting room, between conscious, preconscious, and unconscious: Antonia's first session

Antonia is a young woman of 27, tall, and slim, with a look of deep suffering in her eyes, whose request for analysis stemmed from an awareness of her neurotic condition of unhappiness and inconclusiveness in her relationships and her work. Her life is "stuck", she told me in consultation, "it never gets moving and it never goes anywhere". She lives with her parents – both civil servants – and she herself also works in an office, has a boyfriend and used to be very religious, less so now. She describes herself, spontaneously, as a touchy person, sensitive, and wary, but also sincere and capable of great enthusiasm.

The point – she tells me – is that *she doesn't know what she wants*: she doesn't know whether she wants to live with her boyfriend, or whether she wants to stay on in that office. She doesn't have a clear idea of what her desires are. She knows what annoys her, though, and in general she finds it easier to recognize unpleasant things than desires.

We agree on a four sessions per week psychoanalytic treatment which begins about a month after that first consultation.

Arriving on time for her first session, Antonia greets me in a kind but sober manner, shaking my hand, and as she walks the length of the corridor leading to the consulting room, she looks at the pictures

Representation and syntonization

on the walls. I notice that her gaze is drawn for a moment, in passing, to a small 19th century print showing a hilltop church (one of a series of prints which are dear to me, as they depict the area my family comes from).

As I mentioned, Antonia is rather tall and slim, and today I notice that there is something almost priestly in her gait.

She enters the consulting room, lies down, and immediately recounts a dream:

PATIENT: "I dreamt that I brought you a church candle, a large one. I was afraid there would be many; there were candles, yes: but only a few".

I am struck by the *sacredness* of the image, which could be connected to the way she entered the consulting room, a little as if she were entering a church.

I also note that expression "I was afraid" and the thought comes to me that for her "church candles", an offering which symbolizes devotion, bear witness to the (perhaps disturbing) presence of other faithful worshippers/patients/siblings in the "church"/analysis. But I decide to wait for associations and remain silent. After a few seconds, she addresses me in a decidedly different, more practical tone.

PATIENT (with an unexpectedly pragmatic air): "doctor, on the subject of payment, do you prefer me to give you the money in cash or by cheque?"

I am somewhat taken aback by the change in tone, register, atmosphere and – at least apparently – degree of depth. Earlier, I had felt as if I was in the hushed shadows of the crypt of a medieval church, and then all of a sudden, I find myself at the cash desk in an office (perhaps the office where she works?). I answer as if I too were, in a sense, *at the cash desk*, and tell her that a cheque will be fine.

Silence.

I wait a while, and then I ask her if she feels there is an analogy between bringing a candle and bringing money for payment: in both cases there is an offering, involving an economic sacrifice…

My mentioning the candle induces her to speak of her past attendance at church, which was an alternative (a rather idealizing, and probably less conflictual one, I would imagine) to the family (it

Representation and syntonization

crosses my mind that, in fixing her gaze on the print of the small hilltop church, she had already been organizing a possible idealizing alternative to the reality of the two of us...).

She says that her parents have always worked "like crazy", and that the parental role was actually performed by her maternal grandparents, who are now very ill. While describing her grandparents' health, she becomes visibly upset, and her voice cracks. She holds it in for a while, then she cries.

At this point I am reminded that candles melt, and that she is now *melting/breaking down in tears*, losing her initial stiffness; but I do not say this to her, as it seems to me to be too direct a reference and too early an acknowledgement of the melting of her narcissistic defence, and I do not know her well enough in terms of her fragility. I also remember that during our first consultation she described herself as "touchy and sensitive".

I do not know whether Antonia experiences the melting of the wax as a kind of *yielding* in contrast to the rigid narcissistic nature which she considers to be a form of *solidity*. In any case, I feel that it is opportune to underline a possible connection, an understandable passage between the idealizing sacredness of the initial atmosphere and the humanization of her feelings, which is proving to be a little conflictual and which seems to have caught her off-guard.

So, I tell her, with a perceptibly associative tone and intentionally speaking in a very general sense (*interpsychic not interpersonal contact*), that "candlelight is faint, yes, but invaluable nonetheless for finding one's way in the dark, and that it helps make things out *if one cannot see clearly...*".

This signals a positive function of the "melting", without over-emphasizing it, and without narcissistically disturbing the patient, who seems to value the hardness (the "not melting") as a positive attribute.

PATIENT (visibly taking a breath): "the church and the sacred have to do especially with goodbyes... I am less religious now, but the thought that some people are going to take their leave, or that they are already going away, frightens me" (pause) "I was practically an only child for my grandparents, and the idea of losing them scares me".

ANALYST (making associations out loud, this time freer associations with less regard for the patient's possible reactions, and still bearing church candles in mind, this time as a source of light): "did you feel that you were *the light of their lives?* ...and perhaps you are afraid of losing that 'light'..."

PATIENT (dryly): "well, I have disappeared (note: to say this she uses an idiomatic expression in Italian which is literally "I am eclipsing myself"). I avoid them...just as I avoided the priest from our parish..."

I also feel that the patient *is eclipsing herself.* Consciously, she is referring to her relationship with her grandparents, but I think that this eclipse also concerns her contact with me (as with the parish priest?) now, and above all her contact with herself, as she feels at risk of melting.

I perceive that I may have gone a step too far in suggesting that she put her feelings towards her grandparents under *far too bright a spotlight,* so early on, in the first session. There was a need for some lingering semi-darkness and a less intrusive analytical candle, not a strong direct light.

I will bear that in mind for the future.

And that was the end of our first session, during which I was put in contact already with a deep complexity:

- the light of the church candles, which offer help and comfort in the dark;
- their initial sacred phallic rigidity, which softens and melts with the heat and the *self-sacrifice*;
- the *flame* necessary to have hope, which is one of the components of idealization that is sometimes neglected (people went to church in *despair* – that is, etymologically, having lost hope – seeking hope in the *superhuman* help of a great parent...);
- the anxiety about the loss of her basic objects (in this case, her grandparents), from which Antonia defends herself by *eclipsing herself* and eclipsing them;
- and, at the same time, the unsettling shadow of her feelings of guilt in distancing herself from them and from her parents, if she invests more in her relationship with her boyfriend and in her own future.

My intuition tells me that fear and guilt will be major players in our work over the coming months and years, and that I will have to be prudent, patient and not expect to *light her and make her melt* (like the church candle) too soon, during our sessions, making her pass from a solid/rational state to a liquid/emotive one. I will have to accept that every now and then she will *dry up* and *eclipse herself* for however long is needed, if I do not want her to avoid me analytically like "the parish priest".

I would like to point out here *three unexpected discontinuities*, which caught me off-guard in the first session and which had a specific communicative value on the unconscious level:

- *her priestly gait*, which I had not noticed during the first consultation;
- *her very brief, attentive pause* (without slowing her pace) in front of the 19th century print of the hilltop church;
- and, conversely, the unexpected *administrative passage to the cash desk*, so detached in tone from the rest of our exchange.

With regard to this last moment, I think that Antonia's return to her parents' home in the evening, during her childhood years, brought about a sudden change of gear and atmosphere in the house, with a very pragmatic and concrete handing over of the management of the child and the organization of the following day; and I imagine that this level of exchange was also maintained in the short time she spent with her parents before going to sleep.

I am interested in this shifting of gears not only in a historical-reconstructive sense, but also for the evident continuity between its assumption as an intrapsychic device and as an interpsychic way of functioning (Green, 2000).

Indeed, in the subsequent months this sudden change of gear came up again, even in the transference and in the *hic et nunc* of the session. In short, I was either a sacred but devitalised object (good and reliable, but old and with little drive, like the grandparents) or I became a stimulating, but dangerous and unreliable object, undoubtedly taken up with my own things (like her parents).

And it is there, in that sudden functional *switch*, in that abrupt change of atmosphere and style, that I think the key may lie to understanding the relationship between the patient's defensive Ego and her Self (Bollas, 1987). Just like when her parents arrived, an internal part of the patient identified with them "fetches the child", "packs her up", takes her home, and completely "detaches" her from the previous situation.

Representation and syntonization

The Self is "put to bed" somewhat hurriedly, by an internal demand that is the product of identifications that replace the patient's subjectivity.

At the same time, the Self is "detached", "packed up", and "taken away" – with respect to the two of us in the session – by her defensive Ego/internal parents, who strip her of the emotion previously shared by the two of us.

In retrospect, referring to the therapeutic process, I also think that the analysis/*grandparents* of the beginnings of this treatment, more expansive, tranquil and relaxed, less exciting, less instinctive and less conflictual, was fundamental for getting started. The *19th century church*, representing a type of complex object, was necessary, and entering it with that gait unconsciously condensed a mixture of need, respect, concentration, fear, desperation and hope.

What had been unconsciously communicated made sense, once more. It is up to us to perceive it, even before we understand it.

The "not thought – represented"

I believe that, at times, we analysts slip into the somewhat pedantic tendency of equating – in an inappropriate, formulaic and almost automatic way – the act of representing with that of thinking, whereas the two do not always coincide. *Representation is often a precursor of integrated thought and creative communication is often situated in an intermediate area between the two levels.*

For example, artists – real ones, who possess the gift of knowing how to give an original representation to their internal worlds and of knowing how to communicate it effectively to others – are often quite unaware of part of what they are communicating.

Several years ago, when I was consulted by a famous director for a film about a psychoanalyst, he was taken aback by my noting some implicit elements he had put into the scenes which conveyed profound and important meanings to the viewer. He had been totally unaware of them during his creative process. And it is my understanding that this happens quite frequently in that field.

On a less privileged and protected level, every day vast portions of humanity "play out scenes" with various forms of implicit communication of their internal issues, without even realizing it. And analysts in their professional practice make themselves open to a shared working through of what emerges during the session beyond the words, to make it thinkable (alone and with others), sayable and transformable.

Does carrying out this work on a daily basis imply that analysts, as such, can really have more empathy than other human beings?

My answer would be yes and no.

Unfortunately, we have daily proof, primarily from our own selves, of how many opportunities for contact and compassion can be missed. In the face of this, our only consolation is to consider the real difficulty of our work, as well as our unavoidable personal limitations of course.

We cannot plan empathy, we are not exempt from truly unconscious identifications, or from transference and countertransference. We often make mistakes due to our own defences and those of others, which not by chance have the power to mislead us. We miss countless opportunities to say something useful or, equally, to refrain from saying something inappropriate.

Nevertheless, I would like to come back again to this rather ambitious definition of the concept of psychoanalytic empathy:

> True empathy is a condition of conscious and preconscious contact characterized by separateness, complexity and a linked structure, a wide perceptual spectrum including every colour in the emotional palette, from the lightest to the darkest; above all, it constitutes a progressive shared and deep contact with the complementarity of the object, with the other's defensive ego and split off parts no less than with his ego-syntonic subjectivity".
> (Bolognini, 2002, p. 137)

There is a clear distinction for me between the casual empathy of the majority of people, largely the result of positive interpersonal dispositions in the moment, and psychoanalytic empathy, which is no less casual in actual fact (*it is an event, not a method!*) but incomparably more complex.

I think it should be recognized that, throughout their long years of training, analysts are taught to create those favourable general conditions which I mentioned earlier and which include that resigned and prudent modesty I accredit to sufficiently experienced and disenchanted analysts: the ones who know they do not know.

Analysts develop a good, but not obvious, tolerance for dealing with what is not logical but psychological, and for not being too surprised if Mr. Hyde unexpectedly appears alongside Dr. Jekyll, despite not having been present at the start of the treatment.

The average analyst usually handles sudden and seemingly inexplicable changes of temperature and atmosphere in the session quite well, even when the underlying reasons are not immediately understood. The analyst accepts that the patient is a complicated, inconsistent person with a simplified image, which is often the case with characters in general, both in literature and in life.

This tolerant acceptance and openness to exploratory developments is possible when the analyst is not deluded about his own (the analyst's) psychic simplicity and coherence *a priori*.

The analyst, unlike most people, takes time to understand more, accepting that he does not know, and it is important to recognize that this is no small thing.

4

INTIMACY AND ITS INTERPSYCHIC EQUIVALENTS

More often than might be believed, institutional issues influence the scientific developments of a discipline.

For several decades now, one of the traditional privileges of the president of the International Psychoanalytical Association has been that of choosing the theme of the IPA Congress. And since that honour fell to me on the occasion of the 2017 Congress in Buenos Aires, after careful consideration of the current developments in psychoanalysis I decided to propose the theme "Intimacy", so that it could be explored and debated at an international level.

Today, I can say that it was a good choice, not only for the quantity and quality of the work presented, but above all for the passion it aroused. It placed under the spotlight (and under reflection) that deeply shared relational dimension which characterizes a large part of contemporary psychoanalysis, and which is being progressively integrated into the classical instinctual dimension.

The following thoughts came out from the notes I produced in my opening address, which are deeply connected to the Interpsychic area.

Intimacy

Etymological roots are ancient containers of meaning and studying them is always enriching and enlightening for psychoanalysts.

Intimate comes from the Latin *intra* ("inside"). *Intimus* ("as far inside as possible") is the absolute superlative of *internus* ("which is inside"), while *interior* ("more inside than something else, but not the furthest inside of all") is its comparative form.

Intimacy is the relational dimension in which the internal worlds of human beings can communicate *physiologically* with one another and exchange contents, feelings, and thoughts. Newborns, at birth, have a total need for (bodily and psychic) interchange with someone who can give them what they need to live and grow.

The physiological fusional phase, the prototype of intimacy, is a fundamental passage in the mother–baby relationship, an absolutely necessary primary experience that builds relational competence and organizes lasting and profoundly vital states of the Self.

We rediscover and recreate equivalent conditions of this gradual passage from *within the mother* to *with the mother* in many phases of the therapeutic process, but the crucial importance of these phases is not always sufficiently acknowledged, in either clinical or theoretical contexts.

In fact, the terms *symbiosis* and *fusionality* (Mahler, 1968, 1972) are still mentioned in psychoanalytical texts in a predominantly pathological sense, for the most part, especially with regard to confusional, fixative, parasitic, and more or less secretly manipulative outcomes; and not in a physiological sense (Pallier, 1990; Bolognini, 2002, 2008a; Fonda, 2000; Bonfiglio, 2018), for the healthy and necessary, constitutive and foundational aspects that correspond to a developmental need and that generate a specific make-up, the subject's patrimony.

On a theoretical level, a broad and balanced position including the various potentially positive (= necessary) and negative (= fixative) aspects of fusionality was put forward by Pine (1990) when, with an open formula, he defined the symbiotic phase as "the critical time for the formation of those merger moments (associated with nursing and falling asleep melting into the mother's body) that occur during the first months" (p. 245).

Even now, however, in some clinical *reportages*, the emphasis is not so much on the fact that this fusional experience was not sufficiently experienced in due time and that, consequently, the ability to re-experience it appropriately at later ages is lacking; rather, what is emphasized is the fact (which most of the time is the obvious consequence) that this experience is sought after, unsuccessfully, with a fixated insistence and in ways unsuited to the adult condition, as is often the case – unwittingly – in many dramatic psychiatric forms.

Intimacy and its interpsychic equivalents

In practice, this anomalous behavioural insistence on the inappropriate and disturbing pursuit of fusionality is sometimes presented, in the clinic, more as the problem *per se* than as a sign of underlying, pre-existing problems, almost as if a classic psychiatric phenomenology prevailed over complex psychoanalytic understanding. This creates unfortunate situations in which the analyst presumes to *make the patient understand* at a logical Central Ego level something that he should, instead, be helping him to re-enter into contact with, to experiment and to work through reparatively at least a little at the experiential level of the Self.

In most cases, highlighting the malfunctioning of the Ego in the session only serves to frighten the patient even more with regard to himself and make him feel fear and anger towards the therapist, with consequent seizing up and further malfunctioning of the Ego, and so on.

In this chapter, therefore, I will turn my attention to the relational *medium* in which the majority of effective analytical exchanges take place: that therapeutic situation, favoured by regression, by the specific setting and by the very rhythms of the analytic work, which we define as "intimacy" and which lays the foundations for being able to bring about profound changes in the internal world and way of living of our patients.

This results from our attention to the relationship, no less than to the drives. And a *specific competence of analysts is* precisely that of *recognizing – and, where possible, interpreting and treating – the profound equivalences* that exist, in a way that is not easily readable by non-experts, *between drive, fantasmatic, and relational elements.*

Unlike other kinds of therapist, psychoanalysts do not focus their attention solely on external behaviours and expressive attitudes, or solely on social phenomena or abstract concepts, as sociologists or philosophers are wont to do. Working with the internal reality of our patients implies also a substantial and potentially creative contact with our own internal reality, and with the shared field we co-create with the other during treatment (Baranger & Baranger, 1969; Ferro, 1994, 1995).

The way we do that is, in my opinion, the core of the most stimulating current developments in Psychoanalysis.

How is becoming gradually more important than *what*, in psychoanalysis: the objects of our exploration (unconscious fantasies, memories, fears, needs, and desires) are crucial, in analysis; but *the complex way* through which we can reach, discover, contact, share, handle, work through, represent, and transform them in the analytic interchange with our patients is more crucial today than ever before.

The way the caregiver treated the infant intrapsychically determines and constitutes the initial pre-subjective and then subjective experience of an individual, corresponding thereafter to the way the Ego will contact and treat the Self for the entire remainder of its existence.

The way, probably even more than the selected contents, characterizes to a large extent the different schools, styles, and techniques that today cohabit and co-participate in our scientific, professional, and educational common ground.

Beyond all theoretical differences, intimacy is, in fact, the dimension which sooner or later characterizes the majority of analytic treatments: the dimension where basic functions, such as object constancy, containment, holding, mirroring, nutrition, sharing, reflexive investigation, mutual recognition, appreciation of preconscious creativity and of the flow of free associations, interpretation, and many, many others, can be gradually experienced and utilized.

In almost all treatments, a symbolic equivalence with early phases of the primary experiences is achieved in the relational modes and in the quality of the exchanges.

Bodily exchanges between internal worlds involve two-directional movements and passages *from inside to outside and from outside to inside*: the interchanges can be nutritive, evacuative, genital, and this entails recognition of desire, need, functional coupling at various levels, fertilization, transformation, etc.

This vital mode of intimate interchange is perpetuated throughout the course of our existence, undergoing partial transformations in everyday life, in the constant, embedded and underground unconscious quest for psychic equivalents of what was corporeal in the pre-symbolic evolutionary phases; or, conversely, in the attempt to substitute what is missing (both in the relationship and in the sense of self) with concrete elements, in the present, during the internal exchange with the other.

Psychoanalysis is – in addition to its many other aspects – the science that studies, treats, and sometimes utilizes these processes, at an intra- and inter-psychic level.

Indeed, people seek intimacy throughout their whole lives – in a more or less conflictual way. We see this in everyday interactions, we hear it in the lyrics of almost every song, we come across it in a dramatic and condensed form in our clinical encounters, during which needs and defences manifest themselves and clash with one other incessantly, fluctuating between opening and closing, between drawing near or withdrawing afar, between contact and detachment.

People create and destroy *occasional micro-symbiosis or fusionality* all the time – mostly without even knowing it – putting their more or less developed skills to use in order to organize their potential for psychic coupling at various levels.

Nevertheless, they need some shared intimacy to nourish, oxygenate, and revive their internal world in a recombinatorial way, even though they often have a tendency to consciously deny that need, especially when their defensive organization orients them towards omnipotent fantasies of self-sufficiency and narcissistic anti-object internal attitudes (as happens, e.g. in the case of anorexia or narcissistic personality disorders).

Natural development provides for passageways *from outside to inside* (and *vice versa*) made up of special tissues: *the mucous membranes*, whose function is to provide an intermediate environment in which interchanges can occur fluidly and in which substances can flow from one subject to another proactively, provided the exchange is desired and accepted by both.

My contribution to this field has consisted precisely in highlighting *the psychic equivalents of these intercorporeal processes* and contextualizing them within the psychoanalytic process, with inevitable repercussions on the theory of technique.

I want to underline that here we find ourselves in a context of events that extend beyond the (albeit important) area of attachment, *since they specifically concern exchanges of internal contents*.

Healthy intimacy is the natural dimension of deep interpsychic exchange, in a shared atmosphere in which each individual can learn to alternate primary and secondary processes without fear or shame, modulating their own regression in harmony with the internal movements of the other.

The analyst positions himself ideally in the interpsychic "places" equivalent to the mucous membranes: there where interpretations, emphases, confrontations, and (verbal) interactions can prove useful or harmful, effective or impotent, acceptable or inadmissible, depending on the individual unconscious intrapsychic preconditions and the relational developments that occur in the different situations; there where the *passages from the "inside" of one to the "inside" of the other* can in fact open or close, loosen or seize up, fluidify or dry up and grind to a halt, regardless of the conscious intentions and theoretical convictions of the analyst.

Of course, there is no guarantee that "intimacy" has to mean something good *per se*, given the possibility that it could be used in an openly destructive or subtly perverse way that could damage or destroy one of the two, or even both of them. Holding the key that accesses the interior of the other could lead to a variety of different discoveries, processes, and outcomes, depending on the quality of the drives of the two subjects and on the real quality of their internal object relations.

Consequently, there is also a risk that after having reached a certain degree of intimacy, an analyst might misuse his power by trying to force an interpretation that is premature or unacceptable to the patient's mind, more out of loyalty towards a "scholarly" Ideal or Super-Ego than to get closer to a mutual intonation with the needs and possibilities of the patient himself.

This can occur in a treatment if the natural *Analyst-Theory-Patient oedipal triangle* is unbalanced: for instance, when the *Analyst-Theory couple* is equivalent to an overbearing and excluding parental couple, which could impede a natural intimacy between analyst and patient; or with an *excessively incestual and symbiotic "mother-child/ Analyst-Patient" couple*, with little or no room for the *Third/theory*, which could produce, more than intimacy, an excess of fusion and consequent confusional promiscuity.

At the opposite extreme, an abstract ideal of scientific, *objective* detachment (the *froideur* hoped for – and perhaps even recommended – by Laurence Kahn, 2014), which should preserve analysts from excessive internal involvement, could impede them from resonating as normally integrated human beings, when contacted (or sometimes impacted) by the multifaceted complexity of their patient's internal world.

There is a limit beyond which the (in itself commendable) goal of objectivity degenerates *tout court* into an unconscious defence of subjectivity; just as, conversely, an excess of subjectivity can alter the way of understanding reality.

That said, we know how the analytic relationship is by no means a normal human relationship, because of the patient's transferential regression and in relation to our own therapeutic mandate and responsibility.

Our capacity to symmetrically co-experience the patient's subjectivity, to share (where necessary) the states of his Self, to put ourselves partly in the shoes of the other, requires a clear and stable a-symmetric internal position of the analyst, open to agreement as well as complementarity, so as to allow the patient to display his internal scenarios in a safe and creative relation. In the same way, we must also consider and explore the dangers of an erroneous, misleading, and potentially damaging intimacy.

Nevertheless, we can say that without having painstakingly acquired some sort of appropriate interpsychic intimacy, real changes will be at the very least unlikely, and the analysis would run the risk of remaining a purely intellectual exercise, played out at a purely neurocortical cognitive level.

However, to be clear and avoid any misunderstanding, I am interested in intimacy in the same way I was interested in empathy and *rêverie*; but I am critical towards *intimism* as I was towards *empathism* and as I am towards a potential *reverism*.

These are imitative scholarly degenerations and any attempt to create intimacy intentionally and actively is doomed to fail, exactly as happened with empathy and *rêverie*.

One could say we *cannot decide to be intimate*: all we can do is accept to begin a presumably long and technically challenging psychic cohabitation with, at the very least, a problematic interlocutor, and we rely on our trained capacity for integration (above all at the level of our *Professional Self*) and on our scientific competence (above all at the level of our *Professional Ego*) for facing such a journey.

But we also know that, just like in any journey, sooner or later continuative psychic cohabitation will entail some form of intimacy. Are we ready and truly available for this delicate relational adventure, beyond our abstract and sometimes split ideals?

Ultimately, like empathy and *rêverie*, intimacy cannot be established in analysis on command or by theoretical decree: it usually requires a series of conditions that appear simple but are actually rather complex, and a shared work to co-construct them, where they are lacking.

It also requires at least one of the two to have had a previous direct experience of interpsychic intimacy, just like in ordinary life: theory can do very little, if the analyst has not sufficiently experienced, in their personal life or during their training, how and when the passage of something from one internal world to the other becomes possible.

A primary example of the psychic equivalent of a corporeal condition in analysis

Nutritional tables dictate that a child of any given age should be fed a certain amount of protein, fat, and carbohydrates each day.

Psychoanalytic technique, which varies so much from one school to the next, has provided different indications about administering interpretations. Many things have changed in recent decades, but it is hard to forget some renowned examples of patients given interpretations based more on the analyst's theoretical convictions than on his attunement to the needs, desires and defensive organization of the patient.

To put it in equivalent terms, there have been cases where the inner child was expected to *eat even if he was not hungry*, even if he had indigestion or, worse still, a stomach ache (that is, even if he was still too preoccupied and disturbed by undigested contents that he could neither metabolize nor evacuate them).

By and large, there is still a tendency at times, in certain supervisions or clinical discussions, to pass judgment that "there is a lack of interpretation here", rather than evaluating whether or not the conditions were suitable for proposing an interpretation to the patient.

For example, in certain supervision cases, it is clear that an analyst who is not sufficiently familiar with the evacuative needs of the patient (often so unrewarding for the analyst's sense of self, which is attacked and denigrated) has a certain tendency to bypass them; and that he feels like an "analyst" only when he is able to formulate and administer his interpretation (with the conviction of having, in any case, celebrated the rite correctly, just like some mothers who simply follow the nutritional tables without perceiving the complex internal condition of the child).

Forcing a content (e.g. an interpretation/*suppository*) inside the other in this way can be the equivalent of a bodily act that is sometimes inappropriate and in some cases even violent: it does not produce anything *interpsychic*, but rather something *transpsychic*, which can severely distance the subject from any belief that he might be able to share intimacy.

The same occurs at a genital level in the event of forced obligation of the partner where there is no desire, or even more so in the case of rape (the *phallus/bayonet*; Bolognini, 2014c).

Analysts are required to understand the incessant deep flow of the *symbolic equivalence between corporeality and psyche*, adjusting themselves accordingly in day-to-day intimate exchanges. As a result, they can avoid the concretism of symbolic equation and develop a shared competence in recognizing *when the (inner) child is hungry* or not, when *he has a stomach ache* or not, and so on. In this way, they take care of what the patient needs, so far as it is possible to do so, until the desire is allowed to manifest itself finally in a liveable dimension with less urgency and drama.

Pathological intimate exchanges

Speaking of profound compenetrations (an expression that lends itself just as easily to exciting fantasies of sexual encounters as to others of an idealizing and redemptive variety) it should be said that we are not necessarily in the presence of something good, vital and creative: we know, for example, how sadomasochistic bonds can produce extremely strong ties that are very difficult to dissolve.

One problem that psychoanalysts encounter relatively often during the course of treatments, in fact, concerns the recognition of the healthy or pathological nature of the bond: if, at the extreme poles of the range of relational configurations, the vital or lethal characteristics of the bond and type of intimacy can be easily recognized, then in the middle, instead, it can be said that there is a *grey area* that is more difficult to read and understand.

I refer, for example, to all those relations characterized by a high degree of attachment and habitual routine that are organized in a concrete cohabitation, and yet in which no significant exchanges of internal contents and no reciprocal transformations are observed: relations in which there is a condition of contiguity, but no real opening up of the internal channels.

To put it in bodily terms, to be translated naturally into their corresponding psychic equivalents, these are *contiguities "of skin", in which, however, "the mucous membranes" of the inward openings remain closed or dried up*: there is cohabitation but each one remains *closed* internally. There can be *contact, but no interchange*. There is a customary familiarity, but no intimacy in the etymological sense.

Many marriages, based on fear of solitude but characterized by a similar fear of internal contact, are organized in this way: they are white psychophysical marriages, in which the equivalence of the corporeal and the relational is entirely manifest and coherent.

The analytical equivalent of these relational regimes is analysis in which the patient regularly attends sessions, speaks, tells stories, and appears to associate but.... absolutely nothing happens! And the analysis can go on like this for years, unless something happens between the two that opens up the access to the internal channels: that is, to real intimacy.

The formal bond is there, but the substantial one (in the literal sense of the passage of physical or psychic substances) is not; *there is attachment, but there is no interchange.*

The "inside" is an excluded and unassailable area, *and the relationship is interpersonal, not interpsychic.*

Intimacy... about what?

Many people are inclined to associate the term *intimacy* mainly with some exciting, erotic closeness; which is not necessarily true, neither in relation to the specific area, nor the depth of the affects involved.

Once, a patient of mine was talking about his sense of unsettling tension which he could not connect to anything reasonable.

This is a rather aggressive, narcissistic man who would proudly resist entering into spontaneous contact with any of his own internal attitudes that are not sufficiently phallic. Nevertheless, we have known each other for many years, we have worked a lot together in analysis, and he basically relies on my respectful closeness. Let me add that he knows where the Kleenex are on the shelf beside the couch.

I know that he knows that I would be ready to connect his current emotional state to our upcoming summer separation (it is July), but I have no intention of mentioning it now, since I feel it would sound obvious and "textbook" in this moment, even if I do believe there is some truth in that connection. After a while, his associations lead him – in spite of himself, I might say – to think about his parents' death some years ago, particularly his father's death, with many concrete memories of that day and with a strong emotional contact.

The patient cries and takes a tissue from the shelf. I say something, to show him I understand. The patient is now openly allowing himself to cry, and he dries his eyes with the Kleenex.

We experience intimacy, sharing a pain.

It is a deep interpsychic and intrapsychic passage, that years ago would have been impossible.

The tension has vanished.

I am aware that it is debatable whether the accent should be placed on the upcoming analytic summer separation as the main fact (considering the memory of the father's death as a sort of defensive shift from our current relational event), or on the summer analytic separation as the transferential factor that creates a more meaningful connection with something deeper still and even more relevant for this person.

Here, I only want to underline how intimacy is the co-created and co-creating condition that characterizes this scene, where the *here and now*, the *there and then*, and the *everywhere* and *every time* coexist and interact in the timelessness of the analysis.

Intimacy and libidinal bonds: between fixation and loyalty

For some years now, in developing an initial observation of human relations in general, I have preferred to start from what works well enough, rather than from pathology, and to then make progressive and disenchanted contact with the painful areas of the various situations.

Based on this criterion, I was able to reflect on an aspect that is undoubtedly obvious, but not entirely so: the fact that in relationships where intimacy is created, it is generally easier to establish a stable bond.

However, as I said before, compenetrations could occur inside sadomasochistic relations, producing extremely strong bonds that are very difficult to dissolve.

Nor does this mean that intimacy guarantees the bond, since we know the infinite reactive vicissitudes of opposition, attacks against the bond and rejection of interdependence which in many cases connote the problematic characters (and consequently the relationships) of many individuals.

Nevertheless, intimacy that allows access to the deeper areas of the Self (in terms of bodily/psychic equivalence) is usually an extremely favourable condition for establishing a continuous and intensely involved relationship for the subjects who share it. This is exactly what happens between mother and child, between partners in a couple and – I hope no one is scandalized by this – between dog and owner, when psychic cohabitation is substantial, continuous, significant, and mutually rewarding.

Popular tradition has always cultivated the custom of ritually sharing some basic natural acts (eating together, drinking together, singing together, accommodating guests under the same roof, etc.) which symbolize the creation of a unifying familiarity, a precursor to intimacy. Sharing these concrete acts symbolizes the joint opening up of internal channels and the creation of regulated fusional conditions. The institutional organization of these moments declares the intention, at least, (albeit, as we all know, very often an illusory and unrealistic one) to create effective and lasting bonds (alliances, reconciliations, joint planning, weddings, etc.).

Bonding and intimacy, understood in a broad sense through the metaphorical equivalents brought into play by these rituals that are all too familiar to anthropologists, have been intertwined for millennia, with alternating outcomes.

Let us imagine an elementary schematic representation of a relational vector.

If we picture a line that connects the subject to the object and that defines the distance between them, we can also represent the centre of gravity of the subject's libidinal and narcissistic investment as shifted more or less towards himself or towards the object.

It is common knowledge that there are people who organize themselves autonomously by keeping the centre of gravity towards themselves, while others (hyper-dependents) shift it so far as to coincide almost with the object, towards which they overreach themselves. Others still (often the healthiest) place it in an intermediate area, with the ability to move in one direction or the other depending on how the relationship develops.

In a dual relationship, *intimacy produces a bond when the centre of gravity of the investment is not held by the subject on himself, but is made to fluctuate and to "dolly" back and forth between himself and the object*; when there is recognition of the goodness of the relationship and gratitude towards the object as a source of satisfaction; and when there develops the ability to care about (feel concern for) the fate of the object.

This bonds a subject healthily to the object and, in more mature stages, a subject to another subject.

Allow me to give a deliberately elementary example, one that is easier to represent (for not so elementary reasons) than other inter-human examples: like many, I loved my dog deeply as a *co-subject*, appreciating over the years the richness, finesse and depth of our psychophysical interchanges, made up of sounds, movements, contacts, looks, and actions/thoughts. An intimacy born and raised through daily cohabitation, of which we were both clearly aware, each of us in his own way. I think this is the main reason why I would never have dreamed of replacing him with another dog, one that was more beautiful, younger or more spectacular, perhaps. *He* was *my dog*!

All the more so, this can happen with our own partners, with our own children and with our own friends: and I stress *own* here.

Intimacy, bonding, belonging and loyalty come together naturally, when things go well enough.

But we also know from Freud that the relationship with the dog does not carry weight, so to speak, or not enough at any rate: it saves us a great deal of relational complications and frustrations, given that dogs are not ambivalent and that the centre of gravity of their investment is tipped decidedly towards us.

Coming back, instead, to our specific psychoanalytic sphere, which is far more complex and difficult, I want to highlight a fairly common recurring statement made by many patients in analysis when the treatment has been going on for some time.

It can happen sometimes in the session that they declare, in what appears to be a reductive, casual and almost incidental way during a sequence of thoughts: "no, I would never change analysts… (pause) can you imagine?!? …. I would have to start all over again and tell my whole story from scratch! …"

This seemingly simple sentence contains a world of communications, in a regime of understated, unwitting ambivalence.

At first glance it seems to affirm something positive in the relationship ("I would never change analysts"), instilling in the analyst himself a gratifying feeling of appreciation for a good bond, and for sharing it.

But in actual fact it downsizes the importance of the intersubjective and interpersonal bond, placing the focus instead on a pragmatic question of information-knowledge (*the analyst as a database*) that takes away a lot of meaning from the relationship. The analyst appears much like a public official, a notary who has a dossier of important information for the patient and helpfully safeguards it, nothing more.

The best part is that some patients express this thought, in the session, with the air of someone who feels sure that the other (the analyst) will happily come to an immediate understanding, along the lines of: "obviously, I know you can get where I'm coming from, and that the two of us understand each other perfectly about this, we share the same thought, don't we?". There is a feeling in the air that the patient expects the analyst to be pleased with this proposed understanding, put forward with the look of someone who has said something clever that can be shared.

Sometimes the patient does not seem to grasp that — instinctively — the analyst's very first countertransference reaction can only be negative, due to his disappointment at feeling relegated to such a bureaucratic and secondary role.

But if, as expected and as hoped, the analyst overcomes this first frustrating countertransference hurdle and becomes aware of the patient's defence against recognizing his own experience of the intense, profound, important — and I would say irremediable — bond that connects him to the analyst and that goes far beyond the function of a *database*, then the music changes.

The analyst can realize that the patient is manifesting a narcissistic bastion that he erects for the precise purpose of not feeling the full effects of the bond; or, in some more benign cases, that the patient is coming to terms with his own reticence about communicating something deeper and more substantial to the analyst.

The patient is unconsciously telling the analyst/Object, in that strange and paradoxical avoidant and partially disparaging way, that he will not betray him, that he will be faithful to continuing the analytical work undertaken, because there is by now a bond based on intimacy.

But he is also telling him, without realizing it, that intimacy is not yet free from deep reserves, that there is still work to be done, because the patient is afraid or ashamed of that growing intimacy and of the bond which would almost inevitably result from it.

5

INTERPERSONAL, INTERSUBJECTIVE, INTERPSYCHIC, AND TRANSPSYCHIC

The reader will undoubtedly notice a fairly frequent tendency, on my part, to use certain conceptual formulae that are dear to me, such as: *equivalents*; *non-confusional fusionality*; *practicability of the Preconscious* and – above all – a differentiated use of the concepts of *interpersonal, intersubjective, interpsychic,* and *transpsychic*.

There is nothing absolutely new in these formulae (except for the *interpsychic*), but what is important, I think, is the way in which these concepts are understood and combined by the individual analyst, up to the point of composing his organic vision of psychic life and therapeutic work. If we want to extend to the theoretical sphere what my friend Antonino Ferro likes to say about clinical work, we could think that each analyst *cooks* complex conceptual representations and formulae in a more or less interesting, nutritious and digestible way and according to his own style (and in this book we are definitely in the realm of *Bolognese cuisine…*).

In the following pages, you will find a series of progressive references, which I hope will gradually clarify the meaning of these concepts.

I began this chapter in this way, because it picks up again and further explores the theme of the exchanges of internal contents between two people, the passage from the internal world of one to the internal world of the other, and the ways in which two human beings are combined, in analysis as in life, preconsciously modulating the perception of the Self and the Non-Self.

A first theoretical starting point can be identified in *Three Essays on the Theory of Sexuality* from 1905, where Freud did not limit himself to merely observing and describing the developmental phases of instinctual drives, but admirably extended his gaze to their psychic equivalents.

It can be said that his interest focused progressively on the process of formation and structuring of the intrapsychic (as a precursor also to studies on character), but that he also laid the foundations for rebuilding the experiential-relational-educational environment in which this process develops from the beginning.

The observation point that I now intend to propose starts from there, from psychosexuality, and essentially promotes the concept of *psychic equivalents* of vital bodily functions and, in particular, of *creative corporeal conjunctions* between human beings. I am especially interested in the evolution of the analytic relationship as a place of rediscovery, transformation, and progress in the capacity to relate usefully and, indeed, creatively with the other, through a *partial non-confusional fusionality*.

I prefer to explore the field of pathology, our traditional area of work, starting from that of physiology.

All healthy and natural interactions (nurturing and being nurtured, giving and receiving care, amorous genital intercourse, etc.) have their psychic equivalents: the quality and mode of these relational prototypes generate and organize the subsequent interpsychic exchanges.

These profound interchanges, in analysis as in life, are often unexpected and spontaneous: they are generated and present themselves above all at a preconscious inspirational level. In many cases, they can organize themselves as recurring and unthought procedural automatisms, which produce *an intra- and inter-psychic style* of the individual (Bolognini, 2008a).

The conscious Central Ego can be present and active and can participate and collaborate in these interchanges, but most of the time it is not the real instigator nor, even, does it act as a particularly attentive inspector: more often than not it is a spectator that is either surprised or just *lets things happen*.

At times the conscious Central Ego can be a well-disposed or even loving spectator, whereas at other times it can stand in the way; and I am aware that this whole matter could be described in more academic or scholarly terms, but that way we would, in my view, lose some of its evocative impact.

Relational quality

The fundamental theme is the quality of the experience lived by the individual when he comes into intimate and meaningful contact with another.

As has been described well (Kaes, 1993; Faimberg et al., 1993; Losso, 2000, 2003), if the interaction between two human beings is violent, disturbing, intrusive or destructive, an experience that is difficult to process, then the interaction will be *transpsychic*: the Self will be violated and the Non-Self will prove to be traumatizing.

The bodily equivalents of this experience could be, for example, being violated, in a non-consensual intrusive or violent manner, by a nipple or a penis that forces the entry channel or replaces it with one that is inappropriate and unwanted by the other; or by a piercing voice that penetrates the head through ears that cannot close themselves protectively; or by an unbearable, traumatic sight, etc.

During sessions, in that moment when the patient enters into contact with us and talks to us, we can sometimes feel whether they are trying to intrude or whether they are trying to combine themselves with us in a liveable and creative way; whether they are trying to exchange something internal, whether they have their mouths closed, whether they are evacuating urethral or faecal contents onto us through their equivalents; whether the attempted intrusion is an act of dominance carried out with pleasure and a certain mastery, or whether it is a desperate attempt to seek refuge and return to the foetal state inside us (the two are completely different: one is related to perversion and the other to an unfulfilled primal need); whether the transfer of experiences is total and evacuative, so that the subject is liberated, or whether at least a part of the experience is retained, in a communicative way, etc.

Analytic work is not a corrective or educational process, but rather a shared exploration of past experience and of ongoing conscious, preconscious, and unconscious experiences, which may allow their recovery, representation, possible reintegration, and further elaboration.

Nor is it a purely cognitive process, since the Central Ego can indeed perform its task by integrating the experiential elements and giving them a connection and a sense; but it is the subject's experiential Self that is the primary recipient and the essential co-protagonist of many treatments, and the quality of the relationship between the

Ego and the Self is one of the determining factors for the success of the analysis, as it is more generally also for the subject's quality of life.

The *influence of the intrapsychic on the interpsychic and vice versa* (Green, 2000) is an undeniable fact in clinical work and theory; the process of change requires a shared work of patient and analyst, of the cognitive functions of their Ego and the experiential possibilities of their Self.

I will begin this exploration by taking the bend wide, once again, and starting from the description of a scenario that represents, as a metaphor, some aspects of relational co-habitability. It is set against a backdrop of significant structural features of my home city, which foster a very characteristic social scene, facilitated by a truly extraordinary historical and architectural configuration.

In my view, this scenario will help in our understanding of the inter- and intra-psychic aspects of the situations I'm going to present.

On the buses in Bologna

One lady leans forward to another lady sitting in front of her and, without any preamble and without introducing herself, she comments on a minor occurrence that may have caught both their interests (a young lad brusquely pushing his way off the bus, or the delighted face of a little girl holding her grandfather's hand on her adventure into town, or something similar).

The other lady replies with pleasure, tuning into the same wavelength; and so begins a little impromptu dialogue, a casual one, based on the practice of commenting out loud.

This exchange is not based on the blind, disturbed (and often disturbing) interlocution of the psychotic who does not recognize otherness: here, the otherness is clearly recognized, it is just that the possibility of communicating certain considerations, which become the topic of an exchange in an intermediate space, is perceived and taken for granted as implicitly accepted and acceptable, provided that those considerations are sufficiently generic, hopefully shareable in that they are based on common sense, and not intrusive for the other person, even though they may be expressed in a colourful way.

I have found myself fantasizing that Winnicott would have been most amused to observe these little sketches in Bologna, a city that boasts an architectural intermediate space – its 40 kilometres of porticoes – which are neither home nor street and which lend themselves to conversation, by virtue of being neither *inside* nor *outside* in any absolute sense.

But let's go back inside the bus, another potential Winnicottian space.

The object proposed in the intermediate space by the first lady attracts the second lady, who gladly makes herself at home on the same mental and relational wavelength and reciprocates with no misgivings, producing her own expressions of reply, in an interpsychic experiential environment that plays out in a sort of *non-confusional extension of the Self*.

And so begins an "on-the-bus" conversation: which is not a personal dialogue, mind you, because neither lady recounts any details about her own life; but one in which the aim, instead, is to declare thoughts and feelings of shareable experimentability, both of them taking care not to spill over beyond the bounds of *that intermediate space in which the Self and the Non-Self do not ask to see one another's passport.*

So, the world becomes slightly more co-habitable and ultimately more liveable; the conversation lasts for a few stops (usually along the diagonal streets that criss-cross the city centre) and at the end of the line, the first lady to get off the bus will politely bid farewell to the other, but without exchanging names and most likely without remembering any of her distinguishing features.

They will not greet one another the next time they cross paths, because *these two people do not know each other. They simply shared a limited and intentionally circumscribed interpsychic area,* lasting the duration of a few bus stops. We can see, then, that this was mainly *an interpsychic exchange, not an interpersonal relationship.*

A precursor of the interpsychic concept: "depersonnation"

In a lecture to the "L'Evolution Psychiatrique" group in March 1961 on "the process of the constitution of Ego and Self in the development of the individual, of its structuring function in psychic life and ultimately its disintegration in psychotic states", Paul-Claude Racamier remarked that "odd as it may seem, no word exists to describe such an important process".

He therefore proposed to call this process *personnation*.

Racamier defined *personnation* as "the process by which the human being is able to perceive himself as an individual, as a differentiated, integrated, real, and permanent entity: differentiation, unity, reality, and selfhood are essential aspects of the Self".

With regard to the newborn baby, in which this process is only minimally functional and conditions of well-being are in a psychic state close to sleepiness, Hartmann (1964) and Jacobson (1964) emphasized the *undifferentiation* in relation to the external world as to the internal *milieu*, with investments that are unspecified both in their direction and their nature.

This is the state that, according to Freud, is regarded as the stage of primary narcissism.

It should be noted that Racamier clearly distinguished the well-known psychopathological phenomenon of *depersonnalisation*, defined as a detachment from the live feeling of reality and personal identity, from the phenomenon of *depersonnation*: the pure and simple loss of the sense of Self, the reciprocal of what he defined as *personalisation* (*personnation*).

While *depersonnalisation* involves a pathological degenerative alteration in the perception of self, *depersonnation*, on the other hand, involves a temporary loss of the sense of individuality.

One important difference between the two phenomena that, to my knowledge, has not been adequately remarked upon either by Racamier or by others, emerges from clinical work: *while, in the case of depersonnalisation, patients refer commonly to feelings of violent anguish and perceptions of psychotic experiences accompanying the sense of loss of self,* it can readily be observed how *depersonnation does not for the most part entail such feelings of anguish.*

Depersonnation, instead, is often accompanied by pleasure, or at any rate it defends the subject from pain well enough, appearing in this respect to be a far less dramatic and more effective defence than depersonnalisation.

In other words, the pursuit of some kind of pleasure and protection from pain and anguish can pass through a certain *recovery of undifferentiation*, and therefore through recourse to *partial regressions towards the stage of primary narcissism*, as we see in many group and mass phenomena and in many adolescent situations.

The metaphorical image of the cinematic *"dolly shot"* comes in useful in many cases: how *the individual has the possibility to come and go, backwards and forwards, with respect to these conditions of greater or lesser undifferentiation*, if not deliberately then at least *naturally enough*.

We are not talking, therefore, about a pathological *regressive hole* (see p. 112 in this book), but rather the capacity of the person to *modulate*, on occasion, *their own regressiveness* (and possibly their *regredience*, in the complex sense meant by Botella, & Botella, 2001), to then go on to reorganize themselves at a well-differentiated level recovering their own boundaries and those of others.

The fact that there is a certain dynamic mobility – yet also a certain ambivalence – regarding these movements and these conditions of individuation or undifferentiation is proved, for example, on a popular level, by famously contradictory proverbs that say, on the one hand, "if you want something done, do it yourself"/"too many cooks spoil the broth" but on the other "two heads are better than one"/"many hands make light work"/"there is strength in numbers"; these are all potential and complementary conditions that normally fluctuate in ordinary life.

Humans are political animals; human physiology progressively involves symbiosis, fusionality, the brood, the litter, the family, the group or the team; these aggregations can degenerate into collusion rather than alliance, into family clans, armed mobs or gangs instead of into groups, committees, associations, or parties.

What interests us here is the phenomenon of alternating loss and recovery of boundaries in the experience and the representation of the self.

Naturally, the fundamental text for exploring this field is Freud's 1921 *Group Psychology and the Analysis of the Ego*.

Working together

Segal (1994) spoke about *unconscious cooperation*, starting from the model of sucking.

Gaddini (1982), examining some cases where the patient's narcissism opposed cooperation, described a fascinating and far from rare intra-analytic phenomenon of *clandestine therapeutic alliance*: an alliance that operates unbeknown to the conscious, official and self-representative part of the patient, but that the analyst manages to intercept here and there and utilize without openly declaring it, because, if declared, then the patient's internal parliamentary majority would sabotage this kind of cooperation.

Widlöcher (2003) describes the concept of *co-pensér* (co-thinking) in analysis, a shared associative process which flows not only from patient to analyst but also from analyst to patient, and which depends also on the shared associative context. Strictly speaking, it does not correspond to the transference-countertransference dynamic, nor is it a deliberate technical device; it favours the unconscious communication connecting patient and analyst through a fusional process and a primary identification.

These different contributions shape the functional *We* (including the *working We* in analysis): it is most likely formed there, in the primary physiological fusionality, when that fusionality has been tested and found to function well enough. The *We* has to be rebuilt, instead, when this fusional experience has not been adequately achieved, or has been traumatically "broken".

It is a common experience, in certain analyses, that the happy honeymoon feeling of the initial part of the analysis not only allows the patient to have a good experience right from the very beginning, but it also allows the analyst to work really well: this is not just a feeling, it is something that really happens.

The analyst becomes creative, associates, *produces analytic milk* because in that moment the *interpsychic sucking* process is working; it is an already-experienced experience that is rediscovered and renewed, and this is the happy beginning of many analyses.

In other analyses, however, this beginning is not achieved; we come up against an age-old obstacle and we struggle with the extremely hard task of recreating (or *tout court* creating) an effective reconstituting fusionality.

This is an important part of our work: *putting back together a basic "We"* that coexists with the sense of individuality, allowing this physiological alternation between the sense of individuality and of otherness, on the one hand, and healthy functional *depersonnation* on the other.

Differences between interpsychic, intersubjective, and interpersonal

These three concepts, often used and confused as if they were interchangeable, can overlap in some areas and for some meanings, but they are essentially different.

A *subject* is a human being with a sufficiently coherent self-contact core, capable of experiencing his own feelings and affects with a sense of self-continuity. Functioning in this way is possible when the cohesive perception of the self is present and intense enough, even if the separation process is not completed and the personal boundaries are still scarcely defined; for example, many artists are strongly subjective in spite of a low definition – at least partially – of their boundaries as persons.

A *person* is a human being with a well-defined identity, with very clear physical and psychic boundaries in self-representation, and with a clear psychic distinction from the other. A sufficient part of his mental activity can be developed at a conscious level, with all the limits and defences that psychoanalysis has explored of course.

A person can be defined as such even when he has a tenuous contact with his own subjectivity, as happens in many neuroses. For example, a man and a woman can have sexual intercourse with no subjective feelings; here I am obviously using a concept of *person* that is very different from the integrative one described by Lopez (1976, 1983) who used this term to indicate an individual's maturation towards the harmonious integration of ego, narcissistic, and drive components.

In any case, being a Subject does not always amount to being a Person, and vice versa: the two are not mutually exclusive, nor does one guarantee the other.

The *Interpsychic* is merely *a way of functioning* that connects two individuals; *it is not a general and stable structural condition.*

For instance, when a baby is breastfed, there is no declared personal status. There is almost no consciousness and reflexive awareness at the beginning, but there is a natural cooperation between mouth and nipple that allows both mother and baby to *work together* and to exchange (physical and psychic) internal contents through their entry and exit organs coated with membranes (*mucosa*). The membranes are the porticoes, the passageways between inside and outside from the internal world of one to the internal world of the other (Bolognini, 2008a).

I think that these bodily relations, initially experienced with such a low level of awareness, will find their *interpsychic relational equivalents, but also subsequent intrapsychic equivalents above all at a preconscious level*, as happens in the majority of creative processes; this can also be extended to the Conscious, but more often than not as a non-essential addition.

We know very well, though, that the way the Conscious relates – or doesn't relate – with the Preconscious is essential in intrapsychic life: in terms of quantity, quality, and style of the internal relations.

Naturally, among the fundamental gateways to understanding the interpsychic, it is also important to mention the concept of *transitionality*, which allows the *intersubjective common/condominium spaces, the antechamber and day-area of the Self,* to be frequented in a beneficial way, while protecting the nuclear Self from being traumatically invaded by the Non-Self, and allowing sustainable interactions between the two psychic apparatuses, without experiences of reciprocal violation. It should be underlined again how this is true both for the inter- and the intra-psychic.

However, it is also important to specify how the transitional area concerns an intermediate zone between Self and Non-Self. The concept of interpsychic differs from that of *intermediate area*, in which it provides the equivalent – on a psychic level – of the intimate experience of two individuals who come into close contact and who physically compenetrate (nutritive sucking, kissing, intercourse) via access doors to the Self (equivalent to physiological body openings) aimed at allowing exchange in an enriching and non-intrusive relationship. In this case, the limit between Self and Non-Self can be overcome in a beneficial way, allowing the new dimension of the intercourse, at various levels. Furthermore, in the interpsychic, there are *transfers of (psychic) content from the inside of one to the inside of the other.*

How can all this be reconciled and combined with the intermediate area?

I believe that nothing can truly enter inside us in a calm and digestible way unless the Non-Self has first *convinced*[1] us, by remaining stationary in the potential intermediate area in a non-dissuasive way, of its acceptability and digestibility that is of its compatibility with our Self and its transformability into *some part of us*.

The intermediate area allows for this test experience: the object that does not break into there as an unacceptable Non-Self can stay there just long enough to *convince the Self* to include it.

I believe that the author who has delved most deeply into this topic is Bach (2016) in *Chimera*, where he developed a fascinating analogy between these psychic processes and immune-related phenomena.

Bach cited the fact that the antibody responses that cause transplant organs to be rejected vary rather mysteriously from case to case, and seem to be the consequence of a complex series of factors that affect the recipient organism's ability to include within the genomic Self those elements that enter inside it. In short, his hypothesis is that much depends on the condition and disposition of the recipient with respect to Non-Self elements.

My idea is that the transitional area allows a process of familiarization, with the opening of *doorways towards the inside*, towards what can be accepted and integrated, even if it is Non-Self, provided it is experienced as not harmful and not dangerous for the Self. The transitional space can be conceived as a test area in which the alarm generated by the perception of Non-Self can be temporarily suspended.

Moreover, the interpsychic, as can be seen, has nothing really to do with confusion: it involves sharing a *pre-subjective and co-subjective area* of feeling and thought while retaining – on other levels and with non-dissociated continuity – individual ways of psychic functioning, characterized by a condition of good-enough separateness which is experienced but not formalized (that is, not mentalized by the conscious Ego in a repetitively declared way).

Reflections in the clinic

For an intersubjectivist, the interpsychic may constitute a category that is difficult to understand and relatively unfamiliar, because it concerns phenomena of overlapping and coalescence, exchange and sometimes co-operation between areas and functions of two minds, which do not necessarily correspond to two subjects in the strict sense. It concerns a basic functional physiology, in the relationship between two mental apparatuses, which does not necessarily entail constant involvement of the more structured levels of subjectivity (which, as I will discuss later, can also be co-present in a regime of highly complex psychic functioning). Therefore, it is not necessarily the case that, in an analytical phase of significant interpsychic contact, the analyst is able to answer intersubjectively on the basis of a strong cohesion of the Self.

I have witnessed occasional interpsychic exchanges also with schizophrenics; in those cases, the subjectivity was not at all cohesive, and yet it did happen that "the mouth opened" and something could go in and *vice versa*. This event was interpsychic, not intersubjective, nor was there any interaction going on as people, *in a highly personal way* (Greenberg, 2001), with full and formal definition of identities.

Here is a series of examples:

- In analysis, *with a Person* to whom I feel it is appropriate to propose an increase in the frequency of sessions, I might say: "So, Mr. Bianchi: here we are. Do we want to add a fourth session, after we have worked extensively at three sessions a week?" (This is a dialogue between the analyst's Ego and the patient's Ego, in a primarily conscious functional interpersonal regime).
- *With a subject*, I might say: "If we had a fourth session, do you feel that this could help you?" Less emphasis on the borders of identity, more on the subjective experience of the Self. I appeal, in this case, to the subjective experience, without trotting out *Mr. Bianchi*, that is, without formally or officially convening the Person.
- Finally, *in an interpsychic situation*, I might say: "After your comments about feeling hungry, I'm wondering what it might be like to have four sessions a week; has something similar crossed your mind?" (calling the patient to an associative cooperation and to a shared contact with the experience of the Self). This is another way of sharing the porticoes, the membranes and of making them work in synergy.

The interpsychic is a universal and ubiquitous dimension, but it does not presuppose that in that moment the only functional level at work is the one belonging to separate subjects capable of recognizing others, even if it is clear that this level must have been achieved by the subject, as an advanced point of its general psychic development.

In this sense, Teicholz (1999) noted how mother-child or analyst-patient interactions entail *constant reciprocal regulation, but not necessarily continual, explicit reciprocal recognition*: which may even be avoided at times thanks to just such a regulation.

The interpsychic may, therefore, concern *mobile levels of pre-subjective functioning* and within it, in any case, the patient usually maintains a central position also in the mind of the analyst (conversely, I point out here, with Goldberg [1994], how within intersubjectivism the emphasis often ends up falling on the analyst's feelings, ideas and fantasies during the encounter).

The interpsychic is a level of "wide-band" functioning, in that it allows the natural, uninterrupted and not dissociated coexistence of mental states in which the object (from *ob-jectum*: "placed or thrown forwards") is fully recognized in its separateness, alongside other mental states in which this recognition is more nuanced. This does not occur for pathological reasons, but due to a temporary and transitory condition of *companionable and cooperative fusion* (Bolognini, 1997, 2002; Fonda, 2000) that forms part of the normal, good mental cohabiting of human beings.

It could also be said that, in those moments, recognition of separateness is not necessary: just as when you are boarding a flight, at the gate, the attendant asks you for your boarding card, but does not ask for your passport again.

In this sense, the image of the *cat-flap*, which I dealt with extensively in *Secret Passages* (2008a), comes in handy again as a symbol of something different and intermediate between the opening of the whole and complete *interpersonal door* and the clandestine breaking-in of the *transpsychic cracks* exploited by the mice/pathological projective identifications.

Analysis *constructs a cat-flap and trains the cat* to use it (the cat being a portion of the Ego that is quick at intuitions and associations because it is familiar with, or even coincides with, the Preconscious).

In the interpsychic exchange, we often accept *implicitly, but also instinctively, consensually, and with a significant saving of energy*, that *the cat/conscious-preconscious* enters and exits, which it goes back and forth between us and the others.

At times we see and notice it, at times we do not; its passing is a natural, non-invasive and non-parasitic event that is not subject to rigid control and that generally does not disturb us.

Most likely, this is a crucial part of our "knowing how to get by in this world" and more important than we are normally led to believe.

At this point a rather categorical question may very well arise: when all is said and done, is there or is there not a healthy enough separateness in the relations?

In answering, I think we cannot overlook the complexity of the relationship between subjects, whose effective functional level – in terms of fusion/contact/separateness – is hardly ever univocal. Rather, it is based on a complex coexistence of different organizational modes of the individual and the pair, alternately more or less invested and triggered by developments in the relationship.

Widlöcher's (2001, 2003) concept of *co-thinking* does not imply the loss of individuation; empathy, on the rare occasions it occurs, requires no substantial loss of reciprocal boundaries, but rather a targeted, respectful opening up of contact in specific areas of the Self, suited to the purpose (Fonda, 2000, 2019; Bolognini, 1997, 2002).

As for the relationships between *interpsychic* and concepts that are closely related but to my mind not exactly coincidental, such as *empathy* and *projective identification*, my view is that they describe different aspects of the same homogeneous relational reality.

In short, by *interpsychic I mean a highly permeable functional level shared by two psychic apparatuses*, which facilitates situations of complex empathy through exchanges based on *so-called normal* (Klein, 1955) or *communicative* (Rosenfeld, 1987) *projective identifications.*

Empathy, on the other hand, *is a complex psychic condition, either of the individual or of the pair, which also requires the functional interpsychic levels, but not only these, to be practicable* (Bolognini, 2002): figuratively, *it requires both the cat-flap and the door.*

Projective identification – in the conceptual context we are exploring – is a specific mental and relational operation, which in its communicative forms extensively uses interpsychic levels of exchange (the preconscious cat-flap) and contributes to eventual empathy.

In evacuative or intrusive-parasitic forms, instead, it contributes to pathology and corresponds figuratively to the forced-entry/cracks exploited by the mice (*unconscious parasitic clandestinity*).

In analytic work, it is essential to gradually build confidence in the practicability of shared dialogue with the internal world; the analytic dialogue, experienced interpsychically *from inside*, becomes particularly effective, first in containing and then in symbolizing: what is exchanged may very often be lived out as experientially *true* (as in a dream), even if it is not real.

As for the specific and intentional technical use of the interpsychic, I think that this occurs relatively rarely: it usually requires the analyst to be well-tuned to himself above all else, and then to the patient's internal world and dynamic organization, to enable the transmission of combined verbal/sensory elements from within the analyst to within the patient, in a natural and unforced way.

This should not happen by way of suggestion, but *in a regime of informed consent* towards the patient, that is to say, in collaboration with his conscious Ego, which should become gradually aware of the transformations underway. To make the process more natural and liveable, however, the working pair can occasionally use a *service door on the ground floor* (sticking to the theme of psychic doors), whose key the patient has entrusted to the analyst.

Note

1 "What does 'convince' originally mean? [...] while all the etymology dictionaries have 'convince' as deriving from *cum-vincere*, and unanimously agree that *vincere* (to win) derives from the homonymous Latin verb, the initial *cum-* is instead interpreted in different ways. Some scholars understand it as an indicator of means, or tool: to win through a tool, a means, in a metaphorical sense, and they imply that in any case it is always fundamentally about winning *over* the other. Others, generally conformists, understand it as *winning together, with* the other, as if they were winning in two, in an atmosphere of over-personal search for truth as a value superior to individuals. Still others, openly unorthodox, mock this do-gooder interpretation and make a satire of it: 'If one wins, the other actually... loses!'.

In short, it is on this *cum-* that the interpretations diverge: as if to say that convincing can be an act that produces something good for both or, on the contrary, that if one of the two gains the other will inevitably have to lose, in a sort of reductive version of the famous Occam's Razor ... What we are left with is a sense of persistent ambiguity about the affective and relational nuances of the concept: ultimately, for those who are convinced is there a loss or is there a gain?" (Bolognini, 2017a).

6

SIX COMMONLY USED MINIMAL TECHNICAL TOOLS

As a natural consequence of what we have dealt with up to now, I will go on to describe here some *minimal technical tools* that are widely used by many analysts in a natural and almost instinctive way in their everyday practice.

Unjustly overlooked in analytic literature and considered almost *children of a lesser God*, these technical tools really do seem to pass through the cat-flap, not because they are unconscious, but because they are perceived as essentially and consensually natural in the analytic dialogue. They deserve a mention, in my view, as they are far less obvious and banal than they might appear.

The modulation of the experiential distinction between Self and Non-Self plays a key role in them and characterizes them as interpsychic tools.

"…That is?" (in Italian "…Cioè?") "…such as?" (in Italian "…Tipo?") "…how so?" (in Italian "…in che senso?") requests for clarification

These are questions we habitually ask while patients are speaking, during their associative flow (or non-flow), especially when we feel that something is really missing, or not being said, and so on.

I will mention three very common ones: 1) "That is?" (in Italian "*Cioè?*"), when the patient has said something that is not clear to us. 2) "Such as?" (in Italian "*Tipo?*") This is an intentionally brisk and concise question, aimed at catching the patient's defences off-guard; it is a kind of *extractor of further thoughts* I might use in an attempt to get the patient to work on the descriptive and qualitative aspects of what they are saying, so that they go further, say more and get into the colours, temperature and quality of the experience, and potential similarities with other situations. The third question in this category. 3) "How so?" (in Italian *"In che senso?"*) This is even more mischievous and enigmatic.

These three questions are all further requests for clarification.

To all appearances, this sort of technical tool (let's call it that, since we are referring here to an analytical situation; even if it is clear that these questions are part of the normal everyday dialogue between human beings) seems destined only to stimulate the patient's Central Ego. The patient is spurred on to complete a secondary process that was touched on but immediately interrupted and to clarify the meaning of his reticent, elusive, allusive, incomplete, or otherwise incomprehensible communication. The relational aspect evoked by these brief expressions is actually far more complex.

The object (the analyst) *is animated* and expresses an interest in the thoughts and the feelings of the other. He does not bend to the implicit regime of incomprehension that the subject (the patient) tends to administer to the analyst, just as others had once done to him. The analyst shows he has understood that the patient's defensive Ego is in fact opposing the process of understanding and communication, and he does not passively accept the contract of censorious non-belligerence and functional castration that constitutes this resistance.

Another key point is that these kinds of questions ("That is?" and "Such as?"), which openly and disarmingly reveal the non-omnipotence of the analyst in declaring his inability to understand or know *without the patient's help*, providing the patient with a *direct experiential taste of the strength of non-omnipotence*. Having accepted his limits and the castration of his own illusion of omnipotence ("I know everything, I understand everything…"), he can effectively go deeper into the real situation and the relationship.

Asking, in these cases, is a clear exercise in humility and realism; showing that he knows how to ask intrinsically offers the other (in this case, the patient) contact with the *sustainability of not knowing*, without this corresponding to a disqualifying narcissistic defeat.

Of course, this also entails a partial, temporary surrendering of the *enigmatic status of the object-analyst*, which can sometimes be fruitful both evocatively in the transference and for suspending the analytical work. It should be noted, however, that it is not uncommon for this enigmatic dimension to be emphasized needlessly or even used by the analyst with a – not entirely conscious – secret narcissistic complacency, which allows unnecessary feelings of impotence and inadequacy in the analyst to be offloaded onto the patient.

An expert analyst is *serenely* secure in the knowledge that he knows little to nothing at the beginning, and sometimes even for a considerable period of treatment, and this, paradoxically, is where his strength lies.

This is also one of the reasons why, for example, in the supervision of candidates, we are more interested in understanding what is happening in the development of that particular analysis, asking them to shed light on the reasons behind some of their choices, rather than immediately providing them with pre-established rules or parameters. Those are useful, of course, but we provide them elsewhere usually (e.g., in theoretical seminars) precisely so as not to hinder the exploration of specific and complex events – such as a session – with overly generic formulae.

The patient can experience the analyst's natural and relaxed manner, condensed into a split second, in *dealing respectfully with his own Ego that has not understood*. Overcoming the shame can be facilitated through the direct experience of seeing how the other (the analyst) deals with his own not knowing.

This is not a corrective experience *tout court*, but rather *an experience of how the other deals with his own Self* (Bollas, 1987).

I also want to emphasize that I am not dealing with this aspect from an ethical point of view, but from a technical point of view: not whether it is morally right or not, but what effects it can produce.

The question: "How so...?" has a slightly different specificity. It proposes *an exploratory ulteriority that does not directly charge the patient with reticence*; it asks for something more, an effort, a progressively deeper study with a view to potentially interesting outcomes.

The analyst, in this case, is more openly investigative than overtly unprepared and does not pay a narcissistic price for this request.

Beyond these finer relational aspects, however, the fact remains that in all these cases, the patient is asked to work harder, not to stop on the threshold of the unsaid or the incompletely or incomprehensibly said. The analyst, then, is like a coach who, at the cost of tormenting the pupil, stimulates him to do a better job of representing and communicating.

I repeat: this is not a didactic device, it is coaching; sometimes it is a form of physiotherapy of thought and language.

The patient *is never left in peace,* even if it is for his own benefit.

It is important to keep in mind that it can be a short step from this to being intrusive and persecutory. Every coach should get to know his pupil, reaching the point where he is able to ask him for a sustainable effort without pushing him to breaking point.

Another potentially negative consequence of asking – to watch out for – is the *deflation,* at least to a partial extent, *of the idealization of the object,* which in some cases could turn out to be premature or too brusque. If the analyst (subject/object – supposed to know) asks, it means that he does not know, and this may prove deeply disappointing.

If the idealization of the object is supported and cemented by a powerful narcissistic veneer, the patient may wish to recover the idealized object by turning to another analyst who plays along, stays silent, and never asks, like the aftershave advert from years ago ("For the man who never has to ask!").

The analyst must monitor this potential defensive device of the patient's mental apparatus; the analytic game is made up of subtle perceptions and modulations of *how much reality can be tolerated* (Micati, 1993).

As a final observation, I would note how in many cases this shared reflection occurs on a level of partial symmetry between the two, albeit contained within the frame of asymmetry, of course.

If they are not presented in a superego-like way, *these questions appear to come "from the same height" and not from higher above*; the modulation of sameness and otherness is crucial in this delicate interchange, where it can also occur that the analyst asks the patient: "Help me imagine…".

Using the universalizing impersonal pronoun instead of a personal pronoun

Curiously, it is to Irwin Yalom and his historical textbook on group analysis (1970) that I owe my first interest in this technical device, which he called the *universality of experience* (pp. 26–28). After all, even if the group dimension can evoke a potentially greater sharing of experiences, the pair relationship in the analysis is affected just as much by this process.

As we shall see, the fact that this relational event is commonly found in human dialogues should not make us lose sight of how many specific and not generalizable effects it can produce in analytical work. Sometimes there is a subtle but significant difference between common sense and analytical technique, even if there are interesting areas of overlap, which should neither be denied nor confused.

When we use the impersonal pronoun, we refer to an experiential dimension that is shareable, presenting the patient's experience as potentially extendable to all human beings, as being common to the human condition in general. This limits its apparent abnormality and reduces its characterization as a pathology. One of the deepest fears of many patients is that what they are experiencing is evidence of a severe, incomprehensible, and untreatable pathology.

By using the impersonal pronoun (like when we use the extensive *we*; but the impersonal pronoun is even more diluted and more levelling, humanizing), we make the patient more relaxed about the fact that those psychic experiences, those states of mind are not something that affects only him. They are, at the very least, part of an enlarged human experience and, when possible, also of procedural phases of analysis and of development; or, of *dollying* back and forth between regression and progression.

This has the effect of reintegrating the patient into an implicit area of comprehensibility and helps him to proceed with the work of mentalization and transformation.

The attenuation of the difference between Self and Non-Self, when the impersonal pronoun is used, greatly reduces the anxieties of confrontation, judgement, inferiority, unworthiness, and unacceptability.

The quality of the experience can then be explored in a deeper and more relaxed way; the narcissistic aspects are tempered and made less dangerous and the control of the Ego is made less obsessive: see the expression "Just then 'it' shot!" from the aforementioned book about archery by Herrigel.

With this formula, the impersonal pronoun, there is a skilfully condensed narrowing of the distance between the Self and the Non-Self, between the subject and the object; in this way, we are able to observe a relational event that can be achieved between the two and that stems from a non-intrusive relationship that is not too possessive and not too controlled.

Ultimately, we use the impersonal pronoun at times in the session when it is useful to modulate this universality of experience in a way that is beneficial to the internal functioning of the patient.

Naturally, there can also be defensive uses of the impersonal pronoun, for example, when it is used to deny individual responsibility, in a regime of collusion that has nothing to do with the interpsychic.

"Mmmmh...." as an expansion of thoughtfulness, to facilitate interpsychic syntonization

In 1954, Ralph Greenson devoted a short but intense theoretical-clinical paper to this expression, noting how it corresponds to oral pleasure and how it is connected to the *m* – root of *mother, mamma, mère,* etc.

Greenson dwelt above all on the pleasure aspect.

I would like to call attention, instead, to the experience of *a shared co-thinking contact* (which is not so far removed from Greenson's reference to the pleasure of sucking, of which it is an equivalent) in *a state of non-confusional fusionality*, in which the distinction between Self and Non-Self becomes blurred.

The *"Mmmmh...."* sound is an implicit invitation to share a level of extended reflectiveness, favoured by a pause: it conveys the feeling of a mind at work, with the creation of a space available for thoughts.

It is certainly a less absolute and less disturbing dimension than the *empty void* created by the *hard silence of the analyst* (Bolognini, 2014d), aimed at flushing out the patient's unconscious by destabilizing the defensive Ego and putting it under tension.

There are situations where silence permits the perception and the dramatization of a useful void, open to the exploration of what is new, and where it has an incredibly valuable and profoundly analytical *function of sucking out* the internal contents.

But there are other situations where the analyst's total silence may distance the Self from the Non-Self in a way that is hard to tolerate: it can fragment their contact, freeze or block them, or even send the patient into a panic.

In such cases, the *"Mmmmh...."* sound bears witness to and condenses the analyst's interest, creates an available space for the patient, shows a function of shared thought that may be activated, and provides a functional model, such as: "... do as I do! Try and feel these things, what do they bring to mind for you?"

"Mmmmh...." is basically an invitation: when we use it in a non-stereotypical way, as part of a process of complex perception of the mental state of the other, it can prove a useful technical device.

Noting that the patient has "succeeded in..." or has been "capable of....". The declaration and valorization of analytic progress

This is a tool that should be used in moderation, but whose benefits on the analytic process are extraordinary when the timing is right.

The patient gains recognition for his work and efforts in participating in the analytic process, and for his struggle against the anxieties and resistance that tend to dissuade him from associating in analysis.

The therapeutic alliance is obviously strengthened by this communication, and the patient's sense of self is fortified.

For some patients, this recognition is a veritable balm that soothes wounds inflicted by a lack of appreciation from adults in the past.

Of course, it is important to grant appropriate and realistic recognition, always specific to the patient's analytic commitment, without attributing undue merit, but showing that his work in the session is genuinely appreciated, that it is not a given.

This technical tool is more important than it seems because, basically, both the fundamental rule and what common sense leads us to expect from the patient are taken for granted; in reality, this is not the case at all.

When a patient is able to work in the session, hearing an acknowledgement of that achievement is a source of immense satisfaction and is a positive factor that spurs him on to continue making an effort.

The simple "repetition of what the patient has said" (with the inevitable addition of the analyst's "preconscious resonant nuances")

A brief clinical example can help to illustrate this process.

The patient recounts a dream whose overt content is linked to a news story from the previous day: an Alitalia Airbus had managed to make a daring landing at Rome Fiumicino Airport despite a landing gear failure. Spectacular media coverage and lively collective appeal.

The patient in question is going through a period of difficult and conflictual contact with a negative transference area, whose perception and representation he is resisting because he is afraid of losing a privileged and idealizing idea of his relationship with me, and with the *object* in general.

Metaphorically, it could be said that he is having trouble *landing* on this emotional and relational level and that he would prefer to *fly over* (or skip) it.

PATIENT: "In the dream, I was inside a vehicle, a van perhaps, flying, gliding downwards. I was in the passenger seat. It was clear that we were going to end up in an expanse of muddy, murky, brown water."

ANALYST (slow and rhythmic, with deliberately lengthy pauses, evidently trying out the words the patient blurted out, as if to review together, in slow motion, a sequence that was otherwise too rapid and rushed): Ah! ...so... *the van* ... (pause, perceiving how *the van* might represent something else for the analyst, a generic transference/container vehicle, *for work*) ... glides ... (another pause, highlighting how this could be a gradual and non-traumatic descent, one in which there could be time to think) ... towards *an expanse of brown water* ... (pause; the *water* element recalls a melting in the liquid/fluid nature of the emotions, but the key word here is *brown*, which is emphasized by the analyst as a feature related to dirt) ... *full of mud* ... (pause, to let the growing evidence of the sewer-like/faecal nature of the *plafond* of this representation sink in) ... and you are *next to the driver*.... (pause; this phrase was spoken by the analyst with a sort of curious vitality, as if to show an awakened interest in the relationship) ... who *cannot be seen*, though... (intentionally leaving it hanging, in an obvious way, calling for an inescapable comparison with a feature of the analytical situation, where the patient is *next to the driver, who cannot be seen*)."

PATIENT (laughing, as he perceives an internal transformation underway, which surprises him): "Sure, hearing it repeated like that.... you can't help but think that it was me next to you!"

ANALYST (perceiving, in turn, that the patient's preconscious channels are beginning to open up): "Basically, it's about *landing* without getting hurt... like the people on that plane in Fiumicino...

even if it involves, it would seem, making contact with water that is not exactly…crystal clear!

It appears clear to both of them now, after this interpretation with its amplified resonance, that the patient must *descend* in a bearable way from an idealizing position to one that is more realistic, regarding himself and the object. This involves integrating the negative aspects of the transference as well, which will be represented and examined, if possible, in a gradual and non-traumatic way.

The targeted and intentional use of "we" in specific communicative passages

This tool, aimed at producing functional synergies and sustainable sharing, takes on great importance as an analytic event, as analytic communication, and as an act that is representational of the working pair.

The real *we* is formed in the primary physiological fusionality when this works and can be experienced in a good enough way, paving the way for the gradual definition of *I* and *you*.

In contrast, it has to be rebuilt, with a great deal of patience and without forcing the rhythm and timings, when that good fusionality was not sufficiently formed, or when it has been broken because the subject has been traumatized.

The building or rebuilding of a non-confusional fusionality can, in some cases, be a key part of our work: putting back together a basic *we* that coexists with the sense of individuality. Consideration should always be given, though, to this dynamic physiological alternating between the sense of individuality and otherness on one side, and the healthy partial fusionality on the other.

The working alliance will then be one of the potential benefits of this physiological extension of the Self, the fundamental key to accessing an interpsychic relationship.

In conclusion, these six minimalist technical tools form part of our everyday experience and are pretty much ubiquitous and common to all analysts.

Connected at the interpsychic levels of the relationship, they deserve a mention despite their apparent a-specificity, since, like the *cat-flap*, they help to make our working day less energy-consuming, more natural, and more effective.

7

BEFORE THE INTERSUBJECTIVE

"Presubjective" and "preanalytic" patients in the clinic

Giorgia

Giorgia is what I call *a presubjective and preanalytic patient*.

When she consulted me for a treatment, she didn't accept my proposal to start analysis: she told me that lying on the couch and meeting frequently "from the beginning" (her words) would have been unbearable for her.

So, we have been having face-to-face psychotherapy for one year.

She is *presubjective*, in my opinion, because she has been – and partially still is – occupied and substituted by internal identifications which impede both me and her from being in contact with something authentically *hers*.

On the other hand, she is in my view also *preanalytic*, since I feel she could sooner or later evolve towards an analysis, despite her present refusal and defensive organization.

Here and there, from time to time, she told me about a specific issue with her 3-and-a-half-year-old daughter, who is unable to poop on the toilet in the presence of anyone other than her mother.

So, Giorgia, who works and cannot stay home all day, has to be there and to attend her daughter's evacuations during the night, almost ritually, with no possibility to delegate such an intimate role to the babysitter during the day.

She sincerely regrets that, more as a problem for her little girl, than for herself.

Recently, I noticed Giorgia was becoming more familiar with me and was starting to trust me more.

One week ago, her mobile started ringing during a session; she glanced at the screen quickly and decided to answer, which had never happened before.

"Doctor, excuse me, the babysitter is calling".

It was not the babysitter: it was the little girl on the phone.

She wanted to announce to her mother she had just been able to poop with her babysitter!

Her voice passed beyond the space between the mobile and her mother's ear and reached me: a chirpy, cheerful voice announcing a great achievement, a real conquest, which Giorgia immediately and joyfully shared with her little daughter. A spontaneous *celebration* which I too instinctively joined in with, sharing with an evident facial expression, the general satisfaction that filled our common field in that moment, and that went on for a while also after the call ended.

During this minimalistic episode, I perceived that intimacy was progressing, extending across various interconnected environments: between the little girl and her babysitter, just as between Giorgia and me, and certainly, intrapsychically, between Giorgia's Central Ego and her Self.

All these levels were present and interacted with one other.

I wanted to mention this very basic, but deeply complex and meaningful situation, in order to confirm the many possible aspects and levels of intimacy, and their importance in the evolution of a therapeutic process.

Grazia

In 40 years of psychotherapeutic and psychoanalytic work, I have had only two patients who, while they were talking, automatically shook their heads as if to say "no".

The first, Grazia, I wrote about many years ago (Bolognini, 1991): while telling me that she loved her husband passionately, with an earnest and almost desperate expression on her face, as if she had to convince me of that truth, at the same time, she shook her head no, with the paradoxical effect of unconsciously giving the lie to her own words.

When, two months later, Grazia suddenly cheated on her husband, swept off her feet by having truly fallen in love for the first

Before the intersubjective

time in her life (with another man), I reflected that in that dramatically tense session, two Grazias had expressed themselves: one conscious and intentional, reactively heartfelt and conformist; and the other unconscious, who from inside was sending out a counter-signal, like a prisoner who has devised a trick for getting a message out from prison, through the prison warden!

While "the first Grazia" professed her love for her husband, "the second Grazia" – unbeknownst to the first – said no by shaking her head, meaning: "Don't believe her, *that's not the way things are!*"

Today, I would say that while Grazia was a very neurotic subject initially, she was nevertheless a subject, in an analytical sense. Her shaking her head "no" was ego-dystonic, but her sense of specificity, consistency, and continuity of Self was present and perceptible.

The second patient, whom I will talk about more in detail here, is Renata.

Renata

I have been seeing her face to face (*vis à vis*) for about a year now, in what I consider to be psychotherapy preparatory to analysis and she too, like Grazia, shakes her head "no" while talking. But the effect is entirely different, also because, in her case, the gesture is not sporadic, it is constant, she does it all the time; it is ego-syntonic. It seems to be structured in a stable way by now and – in a clinical aspect that is far from secondary – it has, from the very beginning, had a much more pervasive influence on my own experience.

It took me some time to figure out why I felt so paralyzed, impotent, and irritated when interacting with Renata.

I *was not myself*, from the very first session, and something told me that Renata *was not herself* either.

Renata spoke with great conviction about her husband's "stupid and absurd" behaviour, calling me as a witness to their essentially sadomasochistic goings-on, but more with bewildered disapproval, which I was summoned to share by her explicitly emphatic gaze, than with any pain, an emotion that seemed to find no place or expression in her stories.

On the one hand, the patient drew me into an obvious agreement with her point of view, also given the real eccentricity of the husband whose behaviour in various circumstances seemed deplorable and preposterous, but whom she appeared firmly bound to nonetheless.

On the other hand, she provoked in me a deep frustration as I gradually and reluctantly became a rather impersonal and remote-controlled witness/consultant, overdetermined by her projections, with little or no room for manoeuvre on my part.

Basically, for her, I was a specialist doctor called upon to solve a problem using technical measures for which I should have provided a rational and reassuring explanation, on the wavelength of a constant informed consensus: a *patient Ego/analyst Ego* dialogue (Bolognini, 2002) without any preconscious fishing so that nothing escaped her control.

And still, she carried on shaking her head "no", firmly, looking at me with an air that, over time, I became better at recognising as more authoritative and disapproving than intimidating. It was the air of an adult who shows a silly child that what he is thinking makes no sense, that it has no rhyme or reason; that his ideas or sensations are deeply flawed and that an adult (mother or father) is there to help him understand and guide him towards the correct and appropriate way of thinking.

In short, the head "that said no" served to make the child understand that no, the things he thought or did were not right: *that's not the way to act (or think)!* To the point of replacing his subjective feelings, shifting from a balanced educational function to a real, progressive brainwashing.

What is more, I began to understand (again, a little at a time) that I was made to condense two objects within myself: I was the occasional projective support, the unwilling actor hired to play the part of the *senseless and bad husband/child*, just as, in the heat of an argument, one person uses an unfortunate friend dialectically by lumbering him with the fictional role of the villain: "....What?!?... Are you kidding me?!?... Don't you understand that....etc. etc.", immobilizing him in that awkward position as representing the opponent and forcing him to endure an oppressive and self-referential tirade with no possibility of answering back.

But I also became the *second adult* in a scene played out by several characters, the final witness to the re-education of the child by the *first adult* (interpreted by Renata herself) and all I had to do was confirm and ratify – without a shadow of a doubt – the explanation and the correction of the little reprobate.

Who knows, perhaps I was the father who had to bear witness to the re-education of the daughter by the mother, or *vice versa*; at that

Before the intersubjective

moment in time I still didn't have enough elements to figure it out. What is certain is that I became a parent who had to back up the other parent in that re-education scenario, thus forming an overwhelming majority of "grown-ups" confronting the little Renata of the past.

Naturally, this performance was repeated many times, from one session to the next, only with different pretexts and settings. Imprinted and deep-seated, it was played out as much at an *interpersonal* level (between her and her husband, and only in the second edition between her and me) as at an *intrapsychic* level. This is how her Ego treated her Self, by showing it how foolish and inappropriate it was and how it should be guided back to the right path: "No no no! that's not the way to do it!" (always shaking her head, no).

Where was Renata's Self, her deep Self?

I would add that this type of communication was *far more transpsychic than interpsychic*: my feeling paralyzed and intruded upon by the controlling projective identification of Renata's internal parent who did not allow my Self to exist or to express myself, referred to a probable anal mode of inculcating something in the other by *occupying, substituting*, and therefore *conditioning him*, having forced through his inadequate defences.

In fact, the exchanges did not follow the natural and humanizing pathways of the interpsychic at all.

And so the question arises: *which Renata, or what part of her, were we dealing with?*

When Renata walks into my consulting room, today, I still feel as if I am welcoming a multiple, multi-layered character: an efficient professional woman brings me a not-quite-there, washed-out little girl, who shows herself little and who does not see me.

The one who does see me very well (and keeps me under constant control) is the professional/parent, who every now and then reiterates her request for a technical briefing on how the treatment works and who – I have already had this experience with many other similar patients in terms of internal organization and relational attitude – in difficult moments during her presubjective journey will tell me that "she does not see any results!" A phrase that is so typical, so seemingly legitimate and coherent in a widespread atmosphere of evidence-based scientific validation, but one that in actual fact reveals a critical internal parent at work, who does not aid our work but rather disputes its usefulness by acting as a non-supportive intrusive "third".

For a long time, I have received this condensed and unbalanced *parent-child intrapsychic couple*, trying to tolerate, contain, and calm the predominant internal parent and to help the neglected child/Self to acclimatize and emerge. I define this work as *presubjective*, because the subject – "a human being with a sufficiently coherent self-contact core, capable of experiencing his/her own feelings and affects with a sense of self-continuity" that can function in this way "when the cohesive perception of the self is present and intense enough, even if the separation process is not completed and the personal boundaries are still scarcely defined" (Bolognini, 2016c, p. 11) – is not there yet, or is scarcely there and incapable of expressing itself.

We could cut the theory short, by saying that Renata is a patient in a fairly constant state of identification with a predominant internal object, and therefore that the problem lies in resolving that identificatory defence. This is true to a certain extent, but this formulation does not describe the whole situation in all its complexity.

What is missing is the complementary description of the immaturity, fragility, and non-separateness of Renata's Self, which is like a foetus still in need of a gestational quantum before being exposed to the trials and tribulations of a separated relational contact.

For this reason, the analyst must put to work *also* very complex techniques of prenatal, preseparation containment and nurturing, similar to placental nutrition, which does not require the equivalents of an explicit mouth-to-breast connection; otherwise, the internal parent breaks in and (at the very least) disturbs the process, sometimes even sabotaging it ("….I don't see any results, I'm taking the child away!")

Renata is not a subject yet

The real Renata is still in a presubjective condition, she cannot bear confrontation with the other and she is not even in a condition to be able to use an intermediate area where the distinction between Self and Non-Self is successfully liveable and shareable.

The work is done *from within*, for now, subtly without drawing attention, that is without overly alarming or attacking the despotic internal parent so that *the child is not taken away from me*. The work involves getting Renata used to coming to sessions, to settling in

Before the intersubjective

gradually, to starting an exchange – or more often a negotiation – between me and the pseudo-adult parts identified with the parental object (in a way, the sessions often see me engaged in a rather absurd dialogue with this internal parent/professional Renata).

This clinical strategy allows the deep core of the patient's Self to *inhabit* the consulting room in a liveable way and to grow (at least I hope...) within a sufficiently protected regime, waiting for that first authentic (newborn) squeal and a gaze that sees me, with some emotion. Ours is not yet a true *cohabiting*.

For now, Renata does not see me: she sees a white-coated specialist doctor, who does not really exist.

I repeat: *this work is not intersubjective* (the subject still hasn't appeared yet), *it is interpsychic*, with the addition of that *preobjective placental nutrition* which I will talk about in a later chapter.

It will remain so until Renata has established a sufficiently authentic and constant sense of self, overcoming the massive identificatory state with a pervasive internal object that occupies her and stands between us, and allowing a more real, effective, and consistent self to emerge. At that point, she will evolve towards the condition of the *subject*.

But is it enough to do nothing and wait for this process to unfold? Or are there any further conditions that can help it along? And how far can these conditions be organized technically, or facilitated, or even just appreciated, recognized, and valorized when they occur?

Renata, tomorrow, maybe

Coming back to Renata, I have to say that I am not at all sure this treatment can proceed in the ways and timescales that are needed.

I hope so, and I will do my best to ensure that happens, but I have some concerns about the internal parent's tolerance, which occupies so much space in her and closely monitors our co-presence (I do not feel it can be defined, just yet, as a cooperation). I am also concerned about the mixture of separative idealization/fear/anxiety that is, for now, unconsciously dominant in the patient and that makes it impossible for her, still, to perceive herself authentically and to project herself in a more identified dimension.

Renata seems able, for now, to meet me with a psychic attitude and style that I would define as "outpatient": the analyst should show up wearing a white coat and should function according to protocol.

Before the intersubjective

The analysis appears to be inadvisable for the time being: Renata would not accept it, she has already signalled that by putting up obstacles of every kind (though, in her case, ones that are actually easy to overcome), revealing a deep mistrust, the primitive defence of withdrawing the centre of gravity from the relational axis and – at another level – the fear of betraying the internal parent and suffering retaliation.

Never before, in recent years and in our specific literature, there has been so much talk of the need to *build the analytic patient* (Ogden, 2003; Busch, 2014; Bolognini, 2015a) gradually, given the various kinds of narcissistic and identificatory/substitutive barriers that impede, in the beginning, the natural intake for analytic treatment in the traditional sense, which takes care of the patient's deepest needs.

In the case of Renata, and of many other patients who seem normal, socially adequate and at times even successful but who are in actual fact disturbed and incapable of internal exchanges with the other from within to within, the construction of the analytic patient and the evolution of the person must pass through preparatory interpsychic experiences that nourish the Self. This must take place in a progressive and tolerable way, both from a narcissistic and super-egoic point of view, carefully dosing the perception of the Non-Self while being and remaining alive, we and they, and living together psychically without forcing the timescale of the process.

If these developments take place, the interpsychic nutrition will be able to gradually leave room for the intersubjective relationship, and then for the interpersonal one, adapted to various levels of cohesion and perception of the Self, of separateness and of specific recognition of the self and of the Object.

As often happens in our profession, also with Renata I expect that, if we are able to carry our work forward, one day she might ask me with great surprise if that particular picture or lamp (which have formed part of the *extended-me* in my consulting room for at least 30 years) "…have always been there".

8

PSYCHOANALYSIS AND PSYCHOSIS
Rediscovering the self to rebuild the ego

The theme I will deal with in this chapter is not that of the psychoanalytic treatment of psychoses, on which psychoanalysis boasts a rich and fascinating literature by now, geographically distributed across the three continents (we only need think of the works of Bion, H. Rosenfeld, Searles, Ping Nie Pao, Badaracco, Zapparoli, and D. Rosenfeld, to mention just some of the historical cornerstones). Instead, I will develop a more general observation on current perspectives of psychoanalytic understanding of the alternations between relatively healthy – including neurotic – and psychotic levels of mental functioning.

The analytical work of reconstructing ego functions that have been damaged or hindered by psychosis can be carried out, in many cases, starting from a painstaking and delicate *remediation of the field of the basic relationship*, and from a consequent *indirect, "second intention" repair of the Ego through a reconstituted, liveable experience of the Self*.

This is a current and fascinating topic, which can be approached from *two angles: the psychiatric one*, above all as regards early diagnosis, adolescent-onset psychotic disorders, psychotic breakdown and subsequent compensation strategies in cases with stably structured pathologies; and *the psychotherapeutic/psychoanalytic one*, for the ever improving ability of analysts to identify the functional fluctuations of psychism and object relationality in a broad spectrum, ranging from the full-blown psychotic to the relatively healthy subject, touching on very different and alternating functional levels.

From a strictly psychiatric perspective, according to recent authors (for a review see Van Os and Reininghaus, 2016), an abundant body of research indicates that light, transitory expressions of productive psychotic symptoms (such as delusions and hallucinations), called "psychotic experiences", can be found in the general population with a significant frequency, probably representing behavioural manifestations of a disposition toward psychosis that can be of a genetic, intrapsychic, relational, and socio-environmental nature.

> The majority (about 80%) of people who present these "psychotic experiences" will not suffer from a full-blown psychotic disorder: 20% will continue to report these experiences persistently while about 7% of the latter will go on to develop a psychotic disorder in a structured way.
>
> A sort of bridge is built, therefore, a *continuum* between normality and pathology, and what can be envisaged is a dimensional, non-categorical evaluation of even the most serious symptoms in psychopathology.
>
> (Pazzagli, 2017, p. 103)

This vast clinical reality takes on a great deal of importance also in the field of the prevention of psychiatric pathologies, and it is no coincidence that the area of *adolescent-onset psychosis* has assumed a crucial importance for the purpose of effective therapeutic interventions precisely because they are timely and firmly oriented also in a theoretical sense.

Contemporary psychoanalysis aspires to make a substantial contribution to dealing with this problem, and from my side I intend to examine it in this case from the specific perspective of the relationship between the Ego and the Self (Bolognini, 2008a), exploring some functional connections whose significance has often been overlooked in my opinion.

A first associative *detour* on this vast subject reminds me of the work done with a range of very different patients: from those who would have been defined "psychotic" by analysts but not by psychiatrists (patients who make extensive use of psychotic types of mental functioning, with splitting, dissociations, hyper-projections, pathological projective identifications, autistic retreats, and more or less encysted micro-delusions, but who retain a socially accepted external attitude that is on the whole compatible with a semblance of normality, falling if anything into the *mare magnum* of the borderline category), to those unequivocally and indisputably in need of psychiatric assistance and attention across the board to keep themselves sufficiently compensated; to those branded initially as psychiatric psychotics, who on the contrary regain a calmly effective neuroticism after years of courageous and tenacious work in analysis or – more often – in psychoanalytic psychotherapy.

In short, people whose Ego functioning had experienced significant and evident variations at different times.

A psychotic, not psychiatric, patient

My memory takes me back many years to a patient of mine in his 30s, who was rich, designer-labelled and technologically up-to-the-minute, and who would stop, not far from my office, to talk with a mechanical parrot that dispensed multicoloured plastic balls.

The parrot squawked, in an obviously stereotypical fashion, at any passers-by that set foot within its two-metre radius, inviting them to insert a coin in the machine. My patient answered back seriously, not playfully, striking up an absurd but subdued dialogue that seemed to go unnoticed by other passers-by.

During the session, reinstated to a progressively improved level of ego functioning, the patient gradually came to a realization – at least partially – of the phases of regressive confusion. He and I knew about this psychotic level of his, but no psychiatrist had ever been involved in his life, because on the outside he managed to maintain an appearance of propriety and he did not create problems.

Over time, we also came to establish that the talking parrot was more reassuring and more predictable than me, and it also cost less (considerations that an evolved part of the patient shared with some amusement, but that another part of him, far more deprived, destructured, and vulnerable, did not find funny at all).

Thus, two very different levels of Ego functioning coexisted and alternated within him. Over the years, we learned a lot about the meaning of and the reasons for such alternations.

For example, we learned how our relationship influenced them, at times directly, at other times indirectly; how much ambivalence he felt towards me and in general towards the object; and how his internal contact – at times sufficient, at other times too impaired – with himself and in particular with his feelings was decisive in enabling (or not enabling) his Ego to function adequately.

This work, which lasted for many years with alternating vicissitudes between reintegrative recoveries and regressions to archaic splitting/dissociative operations, gradually shifted the centre of gravity of the patient's internal organization towards greater integration, improving the overall quality of his existence. But it did not entirely eliminate the fragility of its equilibrium in the face of the vicissitudes of internal and external relations. Basically, he felt better and experienced better contact with himself and with the other, but still today I can imagine him regressing in a disorganized and even dramatic way, if faced with difficulties.

An episode of re-integration in a chronic psychiatric patient

As a glaring – and rather astonishing – example that goes in the opposite direction to these alternating functional *défaillances*, I will mention here a patient diagnosed with chronic Hebephrenic schizophrenia who had been hospitalized for 30 years at the St. Clement Psychiatric Hospital in Venice, where he was looked after – with patience and resigned humanity, I must say – by the hospital staff.

This man, elderly now and chronically stable in his severely schizophrenic state, terrified a nurse one day in an acute episode of.... re-integration!

His elder brother had been dead for two years by that stage: he was the one who from the start had come to visit him every week bringing him small treats to comfort him. No one had told him the news, partly because of a lack of confidence in his ability to mentalize the fact and perhaps also for fear of agitating him further.

The patient was described (both in the medical records and verbally by the hospital staff) as an absolutely fatuous and foolish individual, who conveyed a feeling of low intelligence, a particularly unfortunate combination of hebephrenia and mental frailty.

Every now and then he asked after his brother, but in a fleeting, superficial and essentially avoidant way.

The nurse came into my office on the hospital ward, visibly shaken. She had approached the patient's bed to ask him if he wanted his morning coffee, when she felt him grab her hand.

He had stared intently into her eyes with an unnerving "wholeness" and depth never communicated before, and asked her in Venetian dialect: "Maria, tell me the truth: Sergio's dead, isn't he? …"

The nurse was distraught: "Doctor, I've never seen him like this: his mind was all there!"

Then, sadly, everything went back to the way it was before.

That episode remained in the unwritten history of the hospital ward, as a paradoxical and perturbing example of the unpredictability of the human condition in general, but also as one of those events that can terrify anyone who is unprepared (a little like when a patient declared clinically dead suddenly starts to breathe again).

The fluctuation of integrative levels in ego functioning

From experience and by common consensus, this is one of the most intriguing aspects of the psychoanalytic experience, and our vision of the world and human relationships inevitably changes after experiencing and recording, within ourselves, continuous and sometimes important variations in our personal paranoid-schizoid and/or depressive micro-dysfunctions. These variations can include the widening and three-dimensional deepening, or the flattening and shrinking, of our internal space; the invasive and distorting overflow of our projections, obviously conceivable only in retrospect, and the alloplastic effect of projective identifications, so influential on the other, for better or for worse: capable of effectively conveying our thoughts and feelings when they are mainly communicative, and conversely of invading and oppressing the other when they are intrusive, evacuative, or controlling.

And so on and so forth.

In our best moments of self-awareness (i.e. usually during our work, when we are more sensitive and integrated, listening to the other and to ourselves) we are able to connect these variables in our internal meteorology to movements of thought, encounters and exchanges whose importance had been hitherto underestimated, to internal and external events that have touched us, to conditions and even details that determined our state of Self in that moment.

We are able, then, to make sense of our being in the world and our way of working on that day, with a resigned yet confident tolerance towards our functional fluctuations that we bring with us from our training experience.

After all, what is an analyst, if not a person who has learned to recognize and tolerate *a little more than others* the fact of functioning – when all is said and done – *as best as one can*? And is he not – or should he not be – at the same time a person who *trusts himself enough* as regards the possibility of recovering a better functioning, even in the midst of very human alternations and difficulties?

Of course, this is only a very partial aspect of our professional identity, but over the years I have learned to give it the consideration it deserves.

Economic aspects of the "ego-self" relationship

Even if the title of this paragraph may appear inconsistent with the previous considerations, it concerns a possible gateway to the theme of the psychoanalytic approach to psychosis in general, because in my opinion the economic balance is also important as regards the degree of psychic vitality of the subject, which is in turn co-determined at least also by the internal relationship between the Ego and the Self.

Here, I will move primarily in the realm of the *intra*psychic.

My hypothesis is that *the reduction in the energy expended by the defensive Ego, in order to defend us from contact with the repressed Self, allows the Central Ego to work in a better and more integrated way.*

As I already explained in Chapter I, I believe that this economic functional regime does not concern in the same way the defences of repression, on the one hand, and those of splitting and dissociation, on the other, since the latter seem, if anything, to pose problems of a patrimonial nature, in psychic terms rather than in terms of energy expenditure (Bolognini, 2008b).

To achieve a condition of lower energy expenditure at the splitting/dissociation level, we analysts must contribute to *re-familiarizing the Ego with the Self* through analytical work. My hypothesis is that this economic aspect is no less important in the functioning of severe patients than in that of neurotics (for whom traditionally there is a greater tendency to valorize this factor).

I would represent this process with a classic political–military metaphor: it is as if a nation were to scale back its troops at the front so as to have more economic and labour resources internally within its borders; quantitative changes (fewer soldiers at the front and lower costs to keep them stationed there ready for war) in less persecutory and less alarming conditions also produce qualitative changes in the internal life of that nation, which as a whole can become less defensive and more productive.

Subjects with a heavy budget of repression appear stressed, fatigued, and have – so to speak – deep and marked dark circles under their eyes. It is as if they were carrying a very demanding load of suitcases, and this dynamic concerns, above all, the defences against contact with the repressed Self.

Not the splitting and dissociative defences, which in economic terms have no *management costs*, but which entail *losses of capital* (i.e. parts of the Self) that make them impoverished but lighter to bear. They often lack complexity, depth and relational strength, in a word they are *less humanized*.

On the other hand, patients who are very disturbed (but do not know that they are) travel fast, seemingly fresher and – metaphorically speaking – free of hand luggage, *easy going and no problem people*. If anything, they suffer from subsequent persecutory inconveniences when the subject re-encounters in the external world the parts which had been dissociated and separated off far away, and which it no longer recognizes as its own.

These parts will follow him (*persecuzione*; the Latin prefix *per-* from *persequi* has an intensifying and multiplicative value, like *hyper-*) in an incessant attempt to re-enter, in a centripetal way, the place from which they were expelled: that is, the internal world of the subject.

Certain terrors, idiosyncrasies or full-blown delirious or delusional symptoms relate precisely to the Ego's incessant struggle against parts of the Self that persecute it because *they ask* to re-enter.

Re-familiarizing the ego with the self

Let me start by saying that, in this theorization of the unconscious and secret relations of the Ego with the Self, I feel indebted towards Freud and his *Mourning and Melancholia* (1915a), towards all of Winnicott's work and towards Bollas (from *The shadow of the object* [1989] on). More than anyone, in my opinion, they traced a path that allows us today to represent the *relationship between the Ego and the Self of an individual as a condensed intrapsychic functional equivalent of the mother-infant primary relationship*.

In other words, *the Ego tends to treat the Self more or less the same way the mother treated* (in a very general, but above all psychic, sense) *her own child*.

It is often natural for me, in clinical work, to use this concrete example to represent the intrapsychic functioning pattern of many patients: from the style of their *Ego-Self relationship*, I can deduce, fantasize and reconstruct, often usefully and effectively, how they were perceived (or not), treated appropriately (or not) with respect to their preverbal experiences, understood or rejected, narcissistically recognized and valued or ignored and devalued by the primary object.

The work involved in re-actualizing and recreating this fundamental unconscious scene in the analytic story is then experimented intersubjectively and interpersonally by both participants, analyst and patient, at least partially by virtue of *malgré soi*: that is, in an unintentional, unplannable and often unpleasant way. A way that is just as often not analysable in that moment, but only along the way and after the fact.

What is more, this unpleasant reality inexorably erodes those naive omnipotent ideals of an analytic Ego capable of monitoring and instantly interpreting everything it encounters. On the plus side, however, it has the potential to ensure an authentic contact with the Unconscious, as Ted Jacobs (1986) has repeatedly shown in his studies on *enactment*. This is the path I tried to make even more visible and explicit in *Secret Passages* (2008a).

One of the main ways (by now we know there are many...) to guide the analyst's own Ego and that of the patient towards a re-familiarization with the experiential area of the Self passes through the recognition of *psychic and relational – that is, intra- and inter-psychic – equivalents of the bodily exchanges between parents and children* during their upbringing and growth.

The simple description of functions of containment, holding, mirroring, incorporation/internalization/introjection, evacuation/projection, oral/urethral/anal attack, retention, contact, separation, distancing, etc., cannot be truly understood and used *if the analyst does not maintain an experiential and sensorial engagement with the primary biological actions* from which these concepts derive and of which they are equivalents.

A purely abstract, engineered, formulaic, and non-integrated use of these concepts leads nowhere; it becomes an empty litany. And, in these extreme cases that touch on the therapist's internal dissociation, the theory itself can become a fetish rather than a tool.

The analyst must be able to track (cinematic dolly) back and forth at least a little between his own childhood, youth and adulthood, with memories and sensations, to get closer to the patient's experience: "che 'ntender no la può chi no la prova" ("which cannot be understood by one who has not experienced it": Dante, *Vita nova*). At the same time, the analyst must achieve an internal representation of the attitude of the patient's Ego/internal mother regarding those pre-logical experiential levels.

The basic criterion is that each individual treats themselves, in their own intimacy, more or less the same way they were treated *ab initio* by someone else, by a significant and organizing "other".

And this way of treating themselves is condensed within the intra-psychic and – stripped down and rendered interpersonal – within the transference.

Contemporary analysts, pupils of many great authors from the last century and fellows of present-day researchers, also ask *what the patient "is doing", what the analyst is doing, what the two of them are doing*, right in the moment when it seems that, concretely, *they are not doing anything*: they are immobile, talking.

And yet, in a fantasmatic sense, *they are doing something* (Greenberg, 2012).

Compared to the past, it seems to me that nowadays we are less strict about denouncing the energy expenditure of an action in a session (an operation that nonetheless maintains a strong metapsychological sense) as dangerous breakouts away from the representable and the thinkable, and that we are more interested in *understanding the meaning of the equivalents of that action*. Words, even in the absence of any apparent muscular movement, can contain, convey and in some cases even represent action in its purest form.

The old saying "the tongue kills more than the sword" brilliantly summarizes this reality (in this case, an aggressive reality); but, as everyone knows, other intersubjective operations, such as seduction or appeasement, etc., can be carried out with *words that are actions*, due to their meaning, the relational atmosphere they create, their ability to be shared or not, and so on.

In other cases, the action represented and experienced through words is not aggressive, but nourishing and generative; in short, words (and the way they are transmitted) contain and configure interactions; these can be cold or warm, caressing or rough; they produce physical effects, and consequently they induce an advancement or a withdrawal; and so on. In some cases, this is clear and obvious, in others it is not.

Special care must be devoted to the work of understanding the *not-understood equivalents*: those clinical signs of suffering that also indicate natural needs, never considered as such by others or by the patient's own Ego, and which ask to be tolerably *understood* (in the sense of being reassumed internally in a bearable and liveable way) in the Self.

Many clinically spectacular situations of anguish or rage turn out to be the equivalent of *colic in hollow organs due to obstructive tension* and require *a process of loosening and re-canalization of the outflows of accumulated contents*. I leave you to imagine these physio-pathological configurations as their intra- and inter-subjective psychic equivalents.

In these and many other situations of suffering of the Self, the functioning of the Ego is often altered: regressed, intoxicated, projectively distorting reality, darkened and deprived of hope, persecutorily besieged, etc.

More often than not, highlighting this dysfunctional condition to the patient serves no purpose whatsoever; on the contrary, it adds an extra burden of inadequacy to his sense of self.

It is usually more helpful to work on another level, dealing with the patient's Self-states.

The concept of "placental nutrition"

Some severe patients have experienced a disturbed basic object relationship since the time of their first intake with the mother: a *polemical relationship with the object* is thus established.

This category encompasses all those who cannot bear to receive anything from the analyst. The bodily equivalent of this is the refusal to attach to the breast and the need to deny any nutritive dependence on the object. This rejection leads these individuals to a state of proud *relational anorexia* and consequent *libido-emotional cachexia*, which makes the Self suffer and which makes it impossible for the analyst to psychically nourish the patient in the usual ways.

Analytical nutrition then occurs by parenteral, literally *non-oral, equivalents*: it is a containing-placental nutrition that does not involve either the mouth or the eyes of the suckling infant/patient.

The elements of this nutritive method are: *the constant presence of the object; the setting; listening; basic devices for signalling presence and co-respiration* (such as "mmmh!", "that is?" and other technical tools that establish a pre-subjective contact with the patient and that propose the analyst as a pre-object interlocutor); *the "concave" containing-receptive function*, as opposed to the "convex" function that emits something.

In this way, what is entered into is a particular, extremely delicate form of analytic cooperation that has been described by Gaddini (1982) as a *clandestine therapeutic alliance*, which in some way gets around the underlying control and opposition of the patient's narcissism and negative transference.

The case of Alvaro

Alvaro came for a consultation 17 years ago. He was clearly a very disturbed young man, 24 years old, suspicious, and reluctant, not pleased to see me after having been referred by a colleague of mine, who was an old friend of his parents.

I knew from my colleague that Alvaro had recently been hospitalized for several weeks in a private psychiatric residence for persecutory anxieties in an atmosphere of imminent breakdown.

From the first encounter, Alvaro revealed his paranoid organization, saying that my office was near the home of one of his old schoolmates with whom he had quarrelled in the past and who would enjoy seeing him now going to an analyst's office.

However, he also seemed partially willing to speak with me and, after some hesitation, in a few words he said that his father, a famous university scientist, had died when he was twelve years old. He told me that his mother was "stupidly" focusing on collecting antiques instead of funding the travelling he would have liked to do (which made me think, among other equivalences, of his possible image of a psychoanalyst as an annoying "antiquary", more interested in seeking out past memories than in his present desires and his ambitions for the future).

He had tried, unsuccessfully, to study engineering at University but had soon given up after some unpleasant run-ins with "stupid" (again!) professors, who didn't understand his abilities. Then he told me how his previous four-year, three-times-a-week analysis with Dr. S. (a renowned, highly cultured and intelligent colleague whom I greatly esteem) had been a failure, which astonished me.

Finally, he accepted to come once a week for an explorative period, since he wanted to check how we could work together. This could have been my idea too, but it was clear that he wanted to be the one who decided and settled the matter, and it was this kind of initial relationship that characterized the three or four years that followed.

Alvaro would come in and start the session with some very astute observations about details in the room; he would often fish something out from the "minutes" of the previous session or some specific words I had used with him, and draw on this material for long rambling deliberations.

To begin with, his nitpicking bored me stiff. After a while, it prompted me to engage in a series of clarifications much like his, counteracting as if we were involved in some sort of point-scoring contest, competing as to which of us was the sharpest or the most intelligent.

Without connecting it with our contest, he told me how his previous analyst, my esteemed colleague Dr. S., used to compete with him in the same way, in a sort of endless duel of wits that annoyed Alvaro. In fact, I recognized Dr. S.'s style in some of Alvaro's verbal expressions, but unexpectedly also in some of my own at that moment, which were entirely out of character for me!

I was literally *becoming* Dr. S., who had, in turn (besides his personal features and communicative style), inherited Alvaro's father role and relational style in the previous treatment.

Continuing with our *enactments*, Alvaro told me incidentally, without making any conscious connection, about his father's habit of speaking to him in a rather scholarly way, and how he would grant him an audience after dinner in his studio to read and comment on the *Divine Comedy*. His father owned a rare and priceless limited edition of the famous *Divine Comedy*, illustrated by Doré with magnificent drawings, and wanted to share with him every evening a solemn lecture on parts of that sacred text. Little Alvaro objected to this with his whole being.

After a few weeks I became aware of our stubborn repetition and enactment, and this enabled me to change my technical approach considerably.

I gave plenty of room to his speeches without competing with him and without interpreting anything, since when I had actively tried to do something (e.g. connect these intra-session events with his relationship with his father) he reacted very badly, *spitting out* my words.

However, I had also noticed how my interventions had been rejected more for my being active than for their specific content.

Basically, he couldn't receive anything active from me at that time. I had to keep my, albeit admirable, *Divine Comedy*/analytic competence to myself and instead just listen to him, as someone who had a lot to say, but who above all just needed to speak.

Translating this material into its bodily and relational equivalents, it seemed that Alvaro could not tolerate the presence, richness and activity of another separated object (or part of one, such as a nipple, or a phallus, the difference seemed insubstantial). For now, he needed the sessions, but *the feeding had to occur through the placenta, in a fusional, pre-objective condition*; and he needed to speak.

Three years later, he accepted my proposal to increase the frequency of our sessions. I had gone with an off-the-cuff flash of inspiration, suggesting the change in a respectful but encouraging manner.

It seemed important to present it to him more as an opportunity to have more time for listening to him, than as a technical/medical recommendation.

Five years later, he brought some (rare) news about his external life: he had found a rewarding enough job as a computer technician in a company with many other employees.

This was remarkable and surprised me, given his intolerance toward any form of cohabitation. All too soon he came up against some friction here and there with his colleagues, with risk of ruptures in both the job and his internal balance. These reports went on endlessly, with no possibility of intervention, connection, interpretation or even comment by me. Despite this, things went ahead in a progressively liveable way, inside and outside the sessions.

One day he brought me an interesting, famous image: Snoopy lying on the roof of his doghouse (like Alvaro lies on the couch from the beginning) and saying something, with an air of self-assurance, about the Picasso, Renoir, and Van Gogh he has in his mansion.

That was a great moment, since we were both amused by that association, which he openly related to himself with a flash of humour, and which announced a change both in his self-representation and in our relationship, as we shared some interpsychic awareness about that achievement.

At the same time, however, he stopped me in my tracks when I tentatively began to formalize that change by emphasizing the meaning and transference function of that association.

All I had to do was simply receive and silently monitor these passages, including the interpsychic shared awareness, and refrain from any explicit observations.

I was able to work with him interpsychically, but not intersubjectively or interpersonally.

That is, I was able to nourish him, as long as we did not consciously share any subjective comments about his relational experience with me, or any official personal references that would invoke our precise identities.

Seventeen years later, I am still working with Alvaro with the same frequency. His style hasn't changed much from the beginning: he speaks, he tells stories mainly about his vicissitudes at work, while I am now allowed to intervene provided I do it in moderation and with a light touch, sharing – with the utmost caution – even some subjective comments. I can do that now because I spoke little, carefully and softly for years.

What is more, my internal resonance to him and my experiences in the session have changed a lot over the years, and this strikes me as the most significant fact. I now welcome him with pleasure, and I don't feel bored. Quite the contrary, I feel genuinely interested in his life and in what he thinks.

He has grown up in many aspects, he is now a respected technician and manages his job much more calmly and effectively. I know very little about the rest of his life, but on the whole it is clear that he is better in general.

Furthermore, I clearly perceive the deep pleasure he derives from coming to the sessions, even when the content of his associations and his stories has an undercurrent of negativity. The impression is that he *is able to exist* more and more, and that he is able to coexist psychically with me during our work.

Lately, the hypothesis of further increasing the frequency of sessions emerged, in obvious parallel with an equivalent situation at work (the offer to increase the frequency of a certain working collaboration with a colleague, which also raises some doubts for him). We are circling around this possibility, which is in itself significant.

I am aware that one could say, as in many other similar cases: "what?!?... this is not analysis!"

Like many other colleagues (I think), I would reply: "perhaps not. But I am not entirely sure that it is not".

What I do feel sure of is that this is a slow internal transformation of the Object, of the Self, and of the object relationship, which has come about progressively and is still happening. A reconditioning and a work in progress.

I think "Snoopy" is still growing up and perhaps he does not need the Picasso, Renoir, Van Gogh or any other grandiose Self-objects so much anymore, because he now feels less unworthy and less insignificant.

For a long time, I put aside my own analytical *Divine Comedy* and that turned out to be the best thing for both of us; now we have reached a much better level of *psychic cohabitation* in our sessions, even if I still have to be more cautious and more delicate with him than with other patients.

In some cases, this long-term strategy implies an unavoidable phase of treating previously unrecognized primary needs of the human being, when the individual's persistent fragility and residual reactivity prevent him from accepting direct interpersonal analytical nutrition; when it is not yet time for the nipple and its relational equivalents, there is still need for a containing womb and *the nutritional process still has to take place interpsychically passing through an equivalent of the placenta.*

At the level of theory of technique, this raises important questions (of course, related to specific, very severe cases): for example, the risk today of an excessive insistence and emphasis solely on techniques that propose an actively creative containment. The *rêverie* function, which is so valuable and enriching in many cases, can be inadvisable in other cases, when such a functional level is still inaccessible.

We owe to Fred Busch (2019) the most recent, accurate and clear study on this very important concept which understandably captured the attention of many analysts at the turn of the new millennium.

For that matter, forcing a *rêverie*-style dialogue when this is still impossible would be tantamount to expecting an egg to feed on insects and worms with the mother hen, while the embryo still needs to grow and it is the eggshell, first and foremost, that has to protect it and then allow it to hatch.

An old proverb says: "if an egg is broken by an outside force, life ends. If broken by an inside force, life begins".

There is a further danger in proposing a *rêverie*-dialogue too early: that of stimulating in the patient a natural envy towards the analyst, if the patient is still incapable of following him at that pre-separative and pre-subjective level of functioning.

It would be like a premature and humiliating invitation to go swimming, addressed to someone who is still incapable not only of swimming, but also of learning to swim, due to serious impediments.

Sometimes the development of a *rêverie* function is a goal to be achieved after a long period of work, and the analyst should carefully evaluate the condition and ability of his patient to work together at that level.

On the apparent senselessness in the treatment of serious pathologies

Let us return to the torturous scenes of medieval wars, equivalent in some respects to the dramatic atmosphere of severe pathologies which put the interpretative/transformative function of psychoanalysis to the test in new frontier situations: those situations where there often seems to be no thought, and where verbal representation is wholly and traumatically replaced by the act.

In the Late Middle Ages, the western world as it was known then was divided into two great political and military powers in perennial conflict with one another: the Roman Papacy and the Germanic Empire. In our Italian peninsula the former was supported by the Guelphs, the latter by the Ghibellines. The political and military boundary between the two superpowers lay at that time between the cities of Bologna and Modena.

Against this backdrop, in the interminable war between the Bolognese (Guelphs) and the Modenese (Ghibellines), two violent episodes took place within the space of a few days which could capture our attention today not only for their gratuitous brutality, but also for their apparent senselessness.

We are in the year 1325. The Bolognese, while laying siege to a Modenese castle, catapult a live donkey over the walls into the castle, accompanying it with a cacophony of mocking insults and derogatory jeers.

A few days later, the Modenese – who, with the military support of the Emperor, had got their own back on their enemies by defeating them in a bloody battle – march into Bologna through one of the city's gateways, Porta San Felice, massacring the armed guards. In a spectacular move, they steal the famous wooden bucket from the well inside the city walls (the "Stolen Bucket" is the subject of the famous poem of the same name by Alessandro Tassoni, published in Paris in 1622 and then in its final edition in Venice in 1630), returning the insult with a barrage of scornful shouts.

These appear to be harsh exchanges of beta-elements with no sense to them. But it is not so.

By hurling the donkey (which has always been a symbol of poor intelligence and used as an offensive epithet for failed students) over the defences of the hated Modenese, the Bolognese, puffed up with pride in their oldest University in the western world, implicitly landed a blow on them by mocking their boorishness and their cultural inferiority: *"take back into your internal world your asinine nature, and see yourselves reflected in it!"*.

In return and not by chance, the Modenese — the only ones in Medieval Italy who knew how to design and build precious artesian wells — instinctively chose a bucket, a humble, simple but extremely useful bucket, to remind their equally hated cousins of their technological superiority and the inane dependence of others on their skill (that well had most likely been dug and built by those very Modenese technical experts and workers, during peacetime).

This reciprocal traumatic taunting based on violent intrusions therefore made more sense than might at first appear, a hyper-condensed and *thing-like* sense.

Concrete objects and violent acts replaced words, but it seems that the adversaries, in that case, understood one another only too well. Although the elements inflicted transpsychically were the result of vehement action rather than premeditation *in light of the Ego* or deliberate engineering, they nevertheless conveyed implicit, hidden, and hard-hitting symbolic meanings.

As for the dosage between abstract and concrete in human communication, going off on a slight tangent, I am reminded of a good-humoured patient of mine who had solved a problem in her relationship with her boyfriend in a rather brisk and pragmatic — but effective — way (she got him to give her a glittering diamond as a sign of his commitment). In the next session she commented, chuckling at the irony directed at me: "Doctor, in some situations it is good to 'symbolize', sure, but…in a concrete way!!!").

The Middle Ages is (a lot of) water under the bridge, you might say.

Sure. But human nature has not changed that much, beyond and beneath the façade of manners and ideologies.

Once, an enraged borderline patient raised his voice during a session and spat a blasphemous curse at me, his resentment against me bristling and clearly perceptible. Words, sure, but really an action, for the explosive sensorial and emotional impact it had on me, as there was no way I could feel like a mere spectator at the window.

That was a blow, a punch, a transpsychic thump, not an interpsychic exchange. A veritable *"agieren"*, I'd say!

The first problem, with this patient, was that of containing the tensions that had been compressed up until that moment, and then released all of a sudden, with such disruptive force.

In a second moment, however, once the dust from the explosion had settled, we were able gradually to dwell on the incident, to elaborate and analyse the fantasy underlying that specific blasphemy. Indeed, there is a big fantasmatic difference – and therefore a big difference in meaning – between lashing out at the analyst by attacking God or the Madonna respectively. Insults are never levelled by chance against one figure or against the other and the transference framework was clarified usefully, through progressive connections with the specific reviled icon (in that case, the Madonna) and with our relational issues (in that case related to our separation).

After all, in relational traumatisms, the choice of weapon is almost never accidental.

The manifest Unconscious presented with the action can find, in the interpretation and in the *après-coup* psychoanalytic reflection, the understanding of a frequently hyper-condensed sense. It can be stripped of its shell, destructured, associated with something else, recomposed anew and can thus undergo transformations that were entirely inconceivable before.

It can be elaborated, creating meaning, internal space, relation and ability to think.

The concept of "regressive hole"

This empirical concept has always been very useful to me in taking on and treating massive regressive states that dramatically alter the functional performance of the Ego in many patients in post-traumatic situations.

The seemingly paradoxical thing is that *by communicating to the patient the observation that he is in a regressive hole*, and that consequently it is normal and often inevitable that he feels a certain way, *we are working at the level of the Ego* (informing, describing, explaining) *to treat a state of the Self.*

I compare this work to looking at a topographic map together and establishing the position in which we find ourselves: this does not distance us from our current location at all, but it has the fundamental effect of orienting, positioning, giving a place and a meaning to the patient's bewildered experience. This, ultimately, calms him at least a little and gives him hope that he can change his situation.

Years ago, a dear friend of mine told me about a surreal and extremely dangerous experience he had. Wandering through the fields far from his village, he had come across an abandoned farmhouse where there was a ruined well. Leaning recklessly over the edge, to look inside, he had fallen into it.

The well was full of water and it was deep.

Gasping for breath and struggling to stay afloat, he began to scream desperately for help, but it took some time for another person to pass by and peer over the top of the well.

During that interval, his hope had been severely put to the test.

The experience of being perceived in his moment of extreme need, once contact had been made with the person up there, however, insufficient it may have been to solve the problem right there and then, was nevertheless in itself a saving grace. It allowed the anxiety to be contained and, when the emergency services arrived, fortunately the rescue operation was successful.

This (true) story really struck me back then, and I still use it as a metaphor today; it has become a technical tool, which I still make use of today with certain patients, with a natural and firm belief. It allows me to set up a fairly powerful representation of how even Ego-level work ("I see you, I will help you, you are no longer alone, we will work to pull you up") can be more than useful to improve the state of the patient's Self ("I regain hope, I feel calmer, I will do whatever I can to get you to help me") and to help him work in the session.

I have pulled several people up from the well, after administering preparatory *first aid* and giving a sense to their most urgent subjective experience through this metaphor. This corresponded to the exact moment the rope was thrown from the top of the well, way up there, and also helped them to be truly *patient* in the broad sense of the word, allowing the time needed for the rescue operation/therapy to really work.

Primary anxiety and the states of the self

Yet, the most dramatic clinical cases of the *dark ages* are not those swarming with cutthroat and castrating thugs, slaughter, massacres and ambushes, but rather those in which nature becomes the enemy: where the sensory and affective famine, in the primary relationship with an arid or refusing maternal Self, threatens the infant's nascent life. The resulting consequences are reaped both in the quality of the subsequent existence and in the tone of the transference re-actualizations, in life just as much as in analysis.

Frozen or desolate steppes, interminable expanses of deforestation devoid of life, populations wiped out by plagues, fields devoured by locusts, drought and hailstorms, famine and devastation by war, all of these can paint a picture of conditions of extreme solitude with no contact or support in which survival is random and minimal. Just the fact of giving them representation (in dreams, in associations or even just in the images they elicit in the analyst's mind by functional delegation through projective identification) already constitutes considerable progress.

In this, psychoanalysts differ radically from other therapists and from other people in general. For an analyst, the patient's ability to give form to the most deadly and lugubrious scenarios in analysis is already an achievement compared to the absence of thought and representations, and we know how managing to bring them into the session is a significant step forward in the course of treatment. (This brings to mind, staying in the medieval setting, the positive evaluation given by surgeons of the time regarding the *pus bonum et laudabile*, which they knew to recognize as the first sign of improvement in cleaning out an abscess or in the qualitative evolution of pulmonary catarrh).

Where the organicist neuropsychiatrist would immediately use the stopgap of psychopharmacological drugs, without hesitation, to stem his own anxiety even before any manifestations of the patient's malfunctioning and suffering, the analyst would instead start his patient receptive-transformational work: welcoming, containing, exploring, sharing, associating, and gradually giving sense and perspective to the most desperate content.

This is precisely why our work never ceases to appear paradoxical from the outside, also based on this different reading of what a therapeutic process means.

Among these internal scenarios that can become interpsychic, I would therefore include *crossing deserts*: as occurs when the analysis stumbles upon deprived territories of areas of the Self that require a sharing of experience not only to be represented, but also reclaimed and fertilized (Bolognini, 2008a).

The image of the Sahara, once the granary of humanity and now desolately sterile, can return in certain oneiric allegories, but also in certain desperate scenarios of analysis in which *no emotional rain has fallen* for years, given the climate of exhausting *internal aridity* that is shared.

Rare oases allow stunted survival for what remains of the Self: a conflictual tear generated by contact, a smile forced out every now and then, a sporadic subjective comment, a flash of an affect, just to keep from dying.

And so the analyst, no less parched, deprived and emotionally thirsty than the patient, when involved in a necessary and concordant countertransference, becomes an explorer/co-experimenter, substantially making up for the fact that the primary object *was not there* in the moment of need.

Some psychoanalysts have dedicated themselves to the description of these unfortunate conditions.

René Spitz (1965) presented striking sequences of ingravescent neonatal and infant suffering due to object deprivation: from common reactions of crying, to anger, indifferent detachment, depression and finally deadly cachexia.

Anne Alvarez (2017) examined and treated empty passionless states in some patients who seemed to be lost rather than hiding, and inert rather than withdrawn. She wondered: is there a difference between defensive withdrawal and despairing surrender? Do these patients attack the bonds, or do they have bonds that are barely established?

Alvarez clearly differentiates these clinical cases from forms of autistic withdrawal (Tustin, 1981) or from the "psychic retreats" described by John Steiner (1993). Alongside a respectful consideration for genetic factors, the author highlights the importance of relational neglect and the lack of vitality of certain internal objects. Infants necessarily stabilize chronically deprived *Self-states (organized states,* Sander, 1975), which according to Negri begin to be structured as early as the 42nd week in premature babies, once homeostasis has been reached (1994, p. 109).

The basic consequence is that we must try, and try together, to really understand the experience of the other, but above all to share experientially what no one else has ever shared with the subject.

The separation experience in analysis

While psychoanalytic clinical work has thoroughly explored the profound experiences of patients during the *weekend separation,* I am not aware of much having been written about the far more conspicuous phenomenon of the two noteworthy separations that take place during analytic treatment: those for the Christmas and summer holidays.

In my opinion, these two periods of separation present specificities and produce profound effects which differ naturally from patient to patient, but which are common to both periods in a general sense. Let's study them together.

The *Christmas separation* is usually shorter, but it stirs up acute fantasies of exclusion and betrayal, because in that festive season – traditionally devoted to family get-togethers – the analyst is imagined in joyful, exclusive intimacy with his loved ones, in a series of lunches and dinners loaded with emotional significance which distract the analyst and distance him from his relationship with the patient.

It is as if the patients are looking in from the outside, like poor, shivering, excluded children with their noses pressed against the window, observing the unbearable exchanges of gifts and warm embraces inside a cosy apartment inhabited by the analyst's entourage.

What is more, the other traditional celebration in that period, the New Year's Eve Party, exposes patients to another frustration that is hard to bear. Instead of being with them in the session, the analyst will meet another category of loathsome competitors, his personal friends and social circle, together with whom he will happily usher in the New Year with dancing and champagne. This delivers the finishing blow to the patient in full transference regression, making him inclined to represent himself, under the effect of these fantasies, as an epigone of Andersen's Little Match Girl.

I compare the Christmas break in analysis with a sort of very deep crevasse, one which is narrow (being shorter than the summer break) but at high risk of a regressive fall downwards if the patient does not have adequate resources to brave those fantasies.

Conversely, the summer separation – usually a month, but even longer in many cases – is experienced on a deep level as an interminable desert crossing. Here the subjective experience of the patient's Self is not characterized by jealousy or envy regarding oedipal triangulations or other goings-on featuring the analyst as an object to be fought over. The problem is how to survive *tout court* and make it to the other side of the desert or the ocean – that is, to September when sessions will resume – without suffering an excessive depressive depletion and without becoming debilitated in absence of the object.

The regression, during such a prolonged separation, usually suggests primary anxieties more pertinent to the archaic dyadic dimension.

Before and after both separations, however, analysts unfailingly experience the tensions and distancing those patients produce as a response to the event, the reproaches and explicit or covert attacks from which they are not spared even by the most resourceful and well disposed patients. This occurs, for the above-mentioned reasons of transference, even with patients who have a vibrant social life, a fortunate family configuration and who – not infrequently – lead a life that is more fulfilling on the whole than that of the analyst.

But transference and regression make no concessions to anyone during the different phases of treatment, and so it might not hurt for us to revisit these issues, even if they are well known, so as not to forget their inescapable influence on the lives of patients and analysts.

I realize that I have described these typical recurrences of separation in analysis in a rather stereotypical way, slipping into a descriptive vein that is somewhat oleographic. And that I have highlighted the related aspects of suffering, as if they were primarily inconvenient side effects of treatment rather than crucial passages that analysis allows us to revisit and at least partially reclaim, making them more knowable and more liveable.

In reality, like other colleagues, I too am deeply convinced that *after the dream, the transference, the countertransference and the enactment, the crossing of the states of the Self* (Bolognini, 2002, 2008a) is the further psychic and relational event that psychoanalysis will be able to adopt and *transform from an intra- and trans-psychic problem to an interpsychic tool*, gradually giving it a description, theoretical and clinical statute and Baedeker definition, for a definitive and mutative re-introjection within the intrapsychic.

Analysts must be prepared and equipped for these crossings.

Experience has taught me that some deserts can go back to being partially fertile. Of course, this requires the ability to shed a great deal of tears, re-contacting the pain, so as to be able to irrigate and reclaim those arid lands and perhaps even recapture a little joy.

Our work requires us to pass through there, if that is what the patient needs.

This is why I tell students that the *basic concrete elements of the analytic setting* are *the armchair, the couch, and the box of Kleenex beside it*.

Who am I talking to?!?

The famous question posed by Paula Heimann (1950): "who is speaking to whom?" remains one of the key points that enlightens many analytic encounters.

We often find ourselves having a dialogue not with the patient, but with an *identifying outpost* constituted for example by an *internal object with which the patient is in a state of identification* (e.g. the patient's mother or father). That is, with a sort of *avatàr* whose nature remains unknown both to the rest of the patient, who is replaced by it, and to the interlocutor, who instead accepts it as an authentic representative of the person *in toto*.

Incidentally, the etymology of the term *avatàr* (from the Sanskrit *avatara*, adopted in both English and French) is fascinating for psychoanalysts: in Brahmanism and Hinduism, it indicates the descent of a divinity to earth, and in particular each of the ten incarnations of the god Visnù. By extension, in literary use it indicates the reincarnation of a sacred figure, its return, or a *transformation from someone to someone else*. The term then became popular in virtual role-playing games, to denote a character with an array of different features that represents the alter ego of the various participants, taking their place in the actions of the game (*Treccani Dictionary*).

Any experienced analyst knows how often these identifying outposts are inserted between us and the patient's Self, much as if an interfering parent were answering our questions on the patient's behalf.

One of my patients comes to mind, the very rational and refined Letizia, whom I am really struggling to relate to in our sessions.

She speaks impeccably and the things she says are, on the whole, sensible and appropriate, often "nice" and generally witty, and all wrapped up beautifully. However, her slightly gnomic, didactic tone conveys a subtle sense of inauthenticity; her speech comes from *higher up, above* ... I have the recurring feeling that I am speaking *with someone*, not with her. Perhaps with an intelligent and *democratic* mother, very compassionate, agreeable and brilliant, who always rises to the occasion, but not with her.

Letizia describes some examples of irritating behaviour by her children or her husband, whom she treats with intelligent tolerance and with undeniable amusement.

The tone is "... in the end, everything works out fine", and I feel a bit frustrated to begin with, because I do not understand how she can take it all so well, since the premise is there – based on what she tells me – for her not to be quite so serene. Then I feel a mounting rage inside me, rising gradually by degrees.

Little by little, I begin to detest those rather spoiled and tyrannical teenagers, that narcissistic and presumptuous husband who struts about (in Letizia's stories) like a medieval lord, convinced of his own right and obtusely deaf to the needs of others.

And – with an initial twinge of embarrassment toward the residues of my "good-guy" professional Ideal – I feel increasingly impatient with that wise and unfaltering lady, who always has a smile on her face and who looks after the good of everyone. She who reprimands, with cool irony and wit, the daily abuses of others in such a way that those *others* eventually reach a point where they stop those abuses, thanks to a greater maturity inspired by her grace and intelligence.

This wife and mother, at the start of analysis, could have stepped right out of an advertisement, ready to recommend a toothpaste or something to do with wellness, in an atmosphere of unwavering "niceness".

The reality is that Letizia feels terrible and she even went as far as to tell me that, at the beginning, a little fleetingly; but then *that other* inserted itself between us, that marvellous wife and mother who takes care of everyone and who has become her False Self.

The anger I feel is hers. I am a temporary and occasional carrier of an authentic part of her.

She is at least partly replaced by her mother. The internal mother must be gradually recognized and scaled back, in a work of progressive dis-identification.

Sooner or later, Letizia will have to find the strength and the courage to contact areas of her own Self, and consequently to exist and manifest herself, beyond this highly admired and intrusive mother.

In this case, *the patient's Self is largely replaced by a cumbersome and parasitic internal object.*

What are the consequences of this internal organization on the overall functioning of the Ego?

In her case there do not seem to be any energy "brownouts" or states of fatigue (so normal and frequent in classic neurotic patients, busy keeping disturbing representations repressed).

Letizia, on the contrary, seems perfectly fit physically and she carries herself with an enviable verve: a sort of internal fusion with the idealized object redoubles her energy levels.

Right now, however, I notice that this patient, who gives the impression of being so reasonable, has embarked on a series of life decisions and initiatives, which seem to be patently absurd and ill-suited to her and her family members.

As the sessions progress, step by step, it becomes clearer and clearer that Letizia has regulated herself on the basis of the (deplorable, as it turns out) inspiration provided by the idealized internal object: that is, on the basis of what, deep down, she imagines a *marvellous internal mother* would have done.

This is causing her a lot of trouble in her external world, which I will not speak about here.

Letizia's Ego has not been weakened energetically by this state of identification, but rather rendered hypocritical with respect to her usual functional standards (in other sectors and less neurotic moments, Letizia is a very sharp and intelligent woman) and led astray toward goals that are not hers.

The first technical device I have adopted in sessions with Letizia is to take seriously what I am feeling: that is, what a part of her/*not her mother* is feeling – through me.

More than ever, my thoughts turn to Herbert Rosenfeld's (1987) teaching about *remaining perceptive in the session to what we feel moving within us even though it is not ours*: elements that are not ours but that have infiltrated perceptible experiential areas.

Accordingly, in the session I give the appearance of not being attuned to the enthusiasm and the amusement and smug appreciation for the brilliant humour of the patient/ideal mother. *I do not laugh and*, perceptibly, I make a show of *not admiring the enchanting object* that has installed itself in Letizia in place of her Self.

My remaining aloof, *disenchanted* and just short of hard-nosed, gives rise to an initial *feeling of disconnection and doubt* that I sense is disturbing for the patient, who has been used to effectively engaging the other in an immediate and irrefutable collusion in the shared admiration of the idealized object.

Session by session, the patient appears more troubled and less ego-syntonic: she begins to perceive in herself anxieties and dissonance. Flashes of egodystonic irritation towards the husband emerge, some of her children's demands begin to be less obvious, less accepted and, above all, less amusing.

I find myself thinking that this lady's analysis must not seem like a good thing for her family now.

On the plus side, it seems that her ability to read reality and to orient herself by better evaluating the pros and cons of her decisions is increasing in direct proportion with this *process of dis-identification*: it is as if the ability to perceive what is good for her and what is bad for her, what is hot and what is cold, what is wide and what is narrow, etc., is progressing towards a recovery of the experience of her Self, requiring less effort in terms of adaptation towards the Ideal.

The consequences on her ability to do a "reality check" are clear, and Letizia now begins to clash with an unexpected emotional obstacle: the painful difficulty of having to recognize in retrospect how many costly foolish things she has done to make herself feel and appear "wonderful".

I believe it is likely that this progressive change, obtained through the progressive dis-identification from the idealized object and the re-integration of authentic parts of Letizia's Self, will also foster a saving of energy and resources that will benefit the functioning of the Ego.

As I said, this saving is linked to the lesser effort made by the Ego to keep the repression function going (in the case of this patient, to keep the deep-rooted anger unfelt and unthought).

In this specific case, however, what is even more relevant perhaps is the internal identity aspect, which has more to do with *dissociative and substitutive processes of parts of the Self: the alienating identification* (Faimberg, 2005) *with the ideal object has replaced the patient's Self*, and the latter has been partially projected into the other (into me, in the session).

The interpersonal (the patient's relationship with the mother) has become firmly and continuously intrapsychic, with the obvious consequence of assuming a structural consistency and of establishing in Letizia a stable and repetitive intrapsychic neurotic organization.

This brings me back once again to the economic aspect of the issue.

When a splitter device performs an override the energy expenditure is reduced or even zeroed out, and the most important economic element is the loss of parts of the Self. In an economic sense, I compare this to a *loss of capital* (Bolognini, 2008a, 2008b), while in the work of regression there is an energy spending similar to the continuous payment of an expensive bill for utilities such as water, electricity or gas.

A curious detail is that this socially and professionally brilliant patient has made extensive, and by no means banal, use of very primitive defences, which are actually closer to the psychotic than the neurotic pole. Given that her Self has long been largely replaced by an idealized internal object, it would not be wrong to say that *Letizia was, all things considered, quite "beside herself"* (in Italian *"fuori di sé"*, literally *"outside her self"*, means "out of her mind").

And yet her social adaptation was entirely beyond reproach, impeccable almost, and no one in their right mind would have dreamed of considering her a psychiatric case.

9

"UBIQUE ET SEMPER"

Equivalences and consubstantiality between past, present, feared future, and potential future in the analytic experience

In this final chapter, I will attempt to describe something which, in my opinion, is characteristic of the *contemporary analytic attitude, suspended, and fluctuating between diachrony and synchrony*. It is the ability to pass smoothly and easily, back and forth (*with an open return ticket*) among the various time dimensions: the past, the present in the session, current reality outside the session, the repetitive "every time …" of many life situations and the profoundly timeless oneiric reality. All this while remaining in contact with the various functional options of the analyst's psyche as well as that of the patient.

What I intend to describe is something which, I believe, has become more familiar to all of us nowadays, as analysts, producing positive results for our everyday work.

I will then try to connect this temporal aspect, which requires a certain controlled level of *regredience* (Botella & Botella, 2001) in the analyst's mental functioning, with a partial and temporary suspension of the temporal distinctions between past, present, and potential future, to the register of the *equivalences*, which I dealt with extensively in the previous chapters. I will do that by exploring the conceptual area of the *consubstantiality* of much of the Unconscious, that is the partially undifferentiated level at which objects and situations, despite their differences in external reality, share qualitative elements perceived in the secondary process as – indeed – equivalents.

The regredience useful for exploring these levels implies a certain *ability for representational dissolution*, on the part of the analyst, in partially suspending the distinction of perceived differences between objects and situations which are in fact not the same, but which are experienced internally, on some level, as if they were.

Over the course of almost 120 years of psychoanalytic work, the main focus of interpretation has gradually and alternately shifted from the *alibi et tunc* of the reference to the past to the *hic et nunc* of the relationship in the session. That is, from the individual intrapsychic *inside* to the interpsychic past experienced by (and, to some extent, co-created) by the analytic couple, and from the world *in* the session to the world *of* the session. And I would like to extend this as far as the integration of the clinical moment with the fantasmatic undercurrent: that is, *from what is traumatic-precise-historical (right here and only here) to what is repeated-lasting-recurrent in the Unconscious (every time that...)*.

My thesis is that ours is an age of integration, and that *also psychoanalysts' relationship with time*, with the present permeating the past and the past re-presenting itself under new guises, *is evolving towards integration: not only conceptually, but functionally*, as a technical competence.

I would therefore like to integrate the vision of past and present, in the subjective experience of psychoanalysis, with that of the potential future; a future which is sometimes glimpsed, imagined, represented in dreams and in certain anticipatory fantasies, or simply in associations; a future both hoped for and feared, which at times forms part of mental life, and to which we are witnesses or – less frequently – co-interpreters in the analytic setting, *ubique et semper*: everywhere and every time.

In the clinic, we must then reckon with the complex perception of the internal structures and dynamics of each patient, of what can be represented, understood and elaborated throughout the various stages of the analytic process.

I fully agree with Busch when, with admirable acknowledgment of the technical complexity, he writes:

> My proposal is that there is no definite here and now, but only a possible here and now. There is no specific dynamic or content that should have preference over others, but only what is salient

and practicable in the clinical moment. There is no single main route to the healing process in psychoanalysis. The possible here and now is multiple and ever-changing. We sometimes focus on an unconscious fantasy or a defense, a state of self or an objective state, a conflict, both inside and outside the transference. It depends on what is most relevant in that clinical moment. The elaborability of the here and now varies according to the patient's capacity for preconscious awareness.
(Busch, 2014, p. 105 of the Italian edition).

In the discontinuity of subjective experience, I also want to *distinguish* between *what is repeated, what recurs and what is rediscovered/retrieved*.

Naturally, in many cases, this distinction cannot be entirely clear. There are areas of overlapping and confluence between these three configurations, and this must be taken into account on a case by case basis, so as not to over-categorize.

Why can it be important to make this distinction, though? Perhaps to record and recognize, with due caution, the intermediate passages between the deadly and the vital, between the immobile and the evolving, between illness and relative health.

The roots of our most intimate experiences rest on healthy repetitions, recurrences that comfort and ground us, and rediscoveries that reopen games that we had long considered closed.

These events are at the base of individual and collective feelings of identity, familiarity, and liveability of our internal and external world. There is a huge difference, for example, between traditions, with their meaningful rites, and the replacement of our creative psychic movements with sterile obsessive repetitions aimed at suppressing thoughts and feelings.

Let's try to explore this complexity.

Repetition

This life, as you now live it and have lived it, you will have to live once more and innumerable times more, and there will be nothing new in it, but every pain and every joy and every thought and sigh and everything unutterably small or great in your life will have to return to you, all in the same succession and sequence – even this spider and this moonlight between the trees, and even this moment and I myself. The eternal hourglass of existence is turned upside down again and again, and you with it, speck of dust!

Friedrich Nietzsche

The theoretical statute of repetition has undergone various vicissitudes, starting with the famous Freudian text of 1914. *Remembering, Repeating, and Working-Through* is one of Freud's absolute masterpieces, both in content and form. It is a powerful and decisive text, with high theoretical resolution, but relatively short (a characteristic shared by very few other fundamental texts of psychoanalytic literature, Rosenfeld's paper on destructive narcissism [1971] is one example).

Six years later, in *Beyond the Pleasure Principle* (1920), Freud wondered about the conservative nature of drives and the apparent contradiction between the pleasure principle and the compulsion to repeat unpleasant experiences, which led him to venture one step further, postulating a need for repetition connected to the *daemonic* element (a term repeated four times in that text) of the death drive.

The existence of the death drive, and its connection or otherwise to the pleasure principle, would go on to become extremely controversial topics in the theoretical field, after Freud's radical and clearly stated stance in his 1938 *Compendium*. This was Freud in the grips of illness and close to death, his theoretical perspective certainly conditioned by the state of his Self, but still wonderfully lucid in the argumentative functioning of his working ...' Ego.

Later, there would be various attempts to distinguish relatively healthy repetition (at the service of possible re-elaborations of the Ego, such as the *working-off mechanisms* described by Bibring in 1943) from the *repetition compulsion* in its more deadly form; up until the categorical reversal of perspectives proposed by Daniel Lagache (1951, 1953) which replaced the original concept of *need for repetition* with the concept of *repetition of need*.

In my opinion, Lagache's theory, which has largely influenced subsequent generations of analysts, forms part of the trend that I define as *psychoanalytic ecology*. In a positive theoretical sense, it salvages a seemingly entirely negative phenomenon (repetition) by revealing the potentially useful function hidden behind what appears as purely pathological and dysfunctional.

A sort of recycling of waste (intrapsychic and relational, on the clinical level; phenomenological and conceptual, on the theoretical level) which, as we know, has taken place in different eras also through dreams, transference, countertransference and – more recently – *enactment*: these are all circumstances that have been recuperated and transformed from discarded waste or obstacles into potential resources, and finally given the noble status of *via regia* in the technical field.

I must admit that, while I appreciate the spirit of this constructive and ameliorating – albeit maybe slightly optimistic – approach, I do not consider it entirely risk-free, unless it is combined with a suitably disenchanted reality check of the clinical complexity. I think there is a risk, for example, of losing sight of an important aspect of repetition sometimes connected in a truly deadly way with the pleasure principle.

With this I do not presume to take a stand for or against the existence of the death drive, in an absolute theoretical sense.

For example, in our times I believe there is often a tendency to underestimate the importance of the concept of *Fixierung* in its first accepted Freudian meaning, that of 1905 (in *Three Essays on the Theory of Sexuality*). This fixation with more or less secretly pleasurable aspects, perhaps of a sadomasochistic quality, is not always sufficiently taken into consideration, in my opinion, by certain current positions on the theme of repetition. Yet, to me, this seems a somewhat inescapable facet that should not be left in the shadows.

I wonder if perhaps the same turning point in *Beyond the Pleasure Principle* (1920), in which Freud *takes something away* from the concept of libidinal satisfaction to give primary and stand-alone prominence to the repetition compulsion, may have contributed to this partial theoretical obliviousness regarding fixation.

In short, this overly sharp contrast between pleasurable satisfaction and repetition compulsion may be due to underestimating the *secret fixation satisfactions* which are unapparent and paradoxical on the surface and hard to recognize at first glance as, indeed, pleasurable.

A specific aspect of this negative complexity is connected to what I call *secret narcissistic prestige* (Bolognini, 2016b), an over-invested narcissistic trait that takes a long time to emerge in analysis, working underground and producing a barrier (a rock-hard narcissistic glaze, which does not dissolve by lysis) that stonewalls progress in the treatment and the life of the patient.

It is the specific competence of the analyst to recognize and give meaning to these secret pleasures which are hard to see, often paradoxical and ultimately deadly or at the very least harmful, and which do not present reasonable grounds for desirability in the eyes of ordinary people.

Ultimately, what is repeated sometimes unquestionably pertains to the pathological, in a coercive and unresolved dimension that tends towards the deadly. It is no coincidence that we speak of "dead track" in relation to many repetitions that lead nowhere.

I am inclined to think that the supreme, tragic secret pleasure could in many cases be the subversion of the sense of impotence into omnipotence, identifying with the internal aggressor and attacking, punishing and persecuting *with relish* the rejected part of one's Self: *repetition can produce the intoxicating pleasure of identifying with an omnipotent internal object to the detriment of one's own Self.*

In other cases, however, (e.g. in the aforementioned sphere indicated by Lagache, or in that dedicated to "The Myth of the Eternal Return" [Soavi, 1989]), repetition seems to suggest a possible deep vitality in the reappearance of the unresolved, in search of new contactable declensions, of representations that can be metabolized and integrated into the Self, and of different destinies of individual developments (this calls to mind the title of a film: *Play it again, Sam!*).

Clinical examples of repetition are countless, ranging from the most dramatic pole of extreme psychiatric manifestations (such as schizophrenic rocking back and forth) to forms of neurosis in which repetition can condense highly complex underground paths that require a lot of work to decipher.

I cite, among the many situations, patients who keep getting into car accidents, and in particular *those who always turn out to be in the right* as victims of other people's mistakes or culpability, proven every time by witnesses or by police investigation or even by direct admission by the counterparty.

The fervent and documented vindication of irreproachability, on the part of the patient, cannot erase the fact that these circumstances repeat themselves with a certain regularity. And it is not infrequent for analysis to bring to light, over time, background scenarios that led the patient to contribute substantially to the final outcome.

Indeed, in some cases, I have had to disconfirm my initial hypothesis of the driver's lack of empathy towards the driver of the other vehicle, during the manoeuvre, along the lines of "Will he let me pull out as I have the right of way, or will he just speed right on by as if I wasn't there? Right, yes, he's going to let me go!", when that was not actually the case and a collision ensued.

I have come to think, instead, of a paradoxical and complex form of underground empathy in an unconscious part of my patient, capable of tuning in all too well with the likely behaviour of the other driver, contributing to the repetition of a *fixed vindicating script, unknown to the patient's conscious Ego*: "This guy should give me right of way, but he won't. He will behave like my brother who had no respect for my rights. I will prove all of this, bring him to justice and convict him, and I'll make him pay!"

The empathic aspect that I had hypothesized in that repetition therefore had to do with my patient's finely tuned unconscious perception of the casual interlocutor (the other driver, perceived acutely, swiftly, in his oafish attitude) as perfectly suited to represent, on that road, an internal object of the patient himself, converted momentarily without his realizing it into a keenly astute clinician.

Notes on technique regarding repetition

Achille Campanile, a formidable Italian post-war humourist, described (without knowing it) a striking example of *enactment* related to repetition, in his short story entitled *Paganini non ripete* (1974).

To sum it up briefly, Niccolò Paganini has just performed for his part a very difficult piece of music, once again astounding the audience with his virtuosity, and is about to leave the stage after thunderous applause and numerous bows, when an elderly lady in the first row calls for an "*encore*".

Paganini, though visibly flattered, politely and firmly utters his famous axiom: "Paganini does not repeat", which should have ended the matter there.

Unfortunately, however, the elderly lady is deaf and keeps on insisting "*Encore! Encore!*"

The illustrious Paganini does not immediately realize that the lady is deaf, and with a peremptory tone he reiterates that, as everyone knows well, *Paganini does not repeat.*

Being deaf, the lady keeps on insisting, and this gives rise to an increasingly tense and paradoxical situation in which Paganini does not back down from his position of refusal but reiterates it to the point of exasperation and ends up contradicting himself: "Madam, how many times do I have to repeat it?!?... PAGANINI DOES NOT REPEAT! PAGANINI DOES NOT REPEAT!! PAGANINI DOES NOT REPEAT!!!"

Analysts, by virtue of their science and competence, would love to know how to minimize the circumstances of repetition in analysis and nurture the hope of never ending up like Achille Campanile's Paganini.

Inspired by their narcissistic Ideal in its professional form, analysts would like to be able to recognize the signs of (theoretically expected) transference repetition in a timely manner. They would feel like consistent and brilliant analysts if they could highlight it and dissipate it quickly, thanks to the decisive power of a prompt and precise interpretation.

After all, deep down they fear that, if this does not happen, it will spark the instant verdict of the internal analytical tribunal: "the interpretation is missing here!" which is sometimes true, but sometimes not. The problem, in fact, is not that repetition does not take place. It always takes place, as we well know. The point is whether it can be highlighted, recognized, considered, and experienced also on the level of the Self, and whether it is shared between two people to the point of becoming effectively treatable.

The crux of the matter is often the *partial sharing* (that is, not entirely identifying!) *of the experience that is being repeated*, not as a moral duty or virtuous aesthetic posturing on the part of the analyst, but as the only condition that makes it possible to work *from within*, in effective contact with the internal world.

Analysts are experts in this field, however, not because they never stumble into the repetition recreated by the patient's Unconscious, but precisely because they have the tools to experience, recognize, and treat it also *from within*, often in the far from casual and not at all unprecedented scenario set within the analytic framework.

I like to compare one of the analyst's skills to the *Eskimo roll technique* used by expert Kayakers when they capsize in the most torrential white-water rapids. They know how to flip back over through a 180° roll to right themselves: that is their effective specialty, not that of never ending up head-down in the water.

No analyst can hope to go through an analysis without becoming part of a profound repetitive script, and we all know that in theory.

We believe that our ability will be measured in how we manage to pick up on the ongoing situation and make it workable.

But we must also be aware that this implies a narcissistic wound for us nonetheless, because it means that we will not be perfectly in command in certain moments or phases of the analysis. We will not be entirely masters of our own houses, instead we will be – at least partially – cast as extras rather than directors or screenwriters, in someone else's film, where the real director is the Unconscious of the other, even if we retain fundamental responsibilities for managing the execution of the analysis.

We will therefore presumably fall into inevitable repetitions, even with unpleasant and furious head-to-heads like Achille Campanile's Paganini, but with some legitimate hope of working through to awareness, having learned well enough, by trial and error at our own expense, to do the *Eskimo roll*.

And from here, from the area of frank repetition pathology, we can take a further exploratory step towards the partial unsaturated physiology of recurrences.

Let's try to deal with this now.

Recurrences

What recurs falls most often under physiology, part of the natural rhythms of mental, instinctual, and inter-generational events (not trans-generational ones, which are traumatic and do not recur but intrude with repetitiveness like undigested elements and alienating identifications [Faimberg, 2005]).

In recurrences, the unconscious memory seems to manifest a partial, compelling refutation of the principle of absolute atemporality of the Unconscious, and seems to require an equally partial reformulation, as we will see.

In analysis, for example, we recognize and respect the profound cyclic nature of the rhythms of the *setting*, with its seasons and its separations, and the effects that it produces (and let me say that, on average, today's analysts have a greater awareness regarding this than in the past).

That the Unconscious is atemporal is certainly true, but sometimes it is every bit as clear that it is atemporal in its own way: it recalls with relentless precision dates and places that the conscious Ego has lost sight of, and often returns to the scene of the crime (as well as that of the pleasure) without the subject realizing, for a while at least. Maria Pierri (2018) has offered us some valuable essays on this topic.

One example among many is mentioned less in analytical literature compared to other topical dates. The Day of the Dead (2 November), defensively replaced in many countries by the hypomaniacal solution represented by Halloween, often invokes dark and disturbing atmospheres in analysis, which go entirely beyond a conscious contact with memories, losses, pain, and faults related to the world of the patient's family.

Likewise, other dates more specifically connected with the loss of loved ones are often recognized as a source of darkening of the patient's mood only after a certain associative journey in analysis: "I hadn't thought of that". The conscious Ego had not thought of that, but *someone else*, inside, had.

Another common example involves recurrences of significant separations in the *setting*. These preannounce themselves long before the event, in the form of uneasiness, mood swings, in the changing colour of the atmosphere in the session and in the shifts towards situations and figures external to the analysis suitable for representing profound object-related events.

In the previous chapter, I pointed out some very typical specificities in the fantasmatic parade that accompanies the great recurrent separations during the analytic year. In this chapter, I will explore them further from the specific perspective of recurrence, given their predictable seasonality.

The summer separation from the analyst is, in fact, consciously compared to school summer holidays and is often perceived well in advance – and experienced in the field – more or less like crossing a desert. A long absence of the object which engages the patient in a struggle for survival, during which the analyst is goodness knows where. Distances experienced in light years which are preannounced many weeks before in the profound movements and oneiric, fantastic productions in the session, sometimes in the acts and in the counter-defences (like journeys that are somewhat demanding and perhaps even risky, but nevertheless aimed at counterposing a strong "elsewhere" in contrast to "us here", in response to the absence of the object).

The passive abandonment instantly mutates, then, into active distancing, perhaps anticipating the detachment from the sessions and balancing the absence of the object with casual investments in other figures.

Very often *during the great summer separation* the object-analyst disappears from conscious representations ("No, you see, Doctor, I never thought of analysis, not once!") and in any case the patient does not imagine where the analyst is. The overriding fantasy has to do with abandonment, rather than with exclusion. It is, as I said, a *predominantly dyadic dimension*.

Conversely, *the brief but very intense separation for the festive season* triggers fantasies of a completely different nature and could be compared to the depth of a narrow crevasse in a glacier. A few short days, but with immense evocative power. Why is that?

Because, as is common knowledge, the Christmas and New Year holidays involve important family gatherings (Christmas Eve, Christmas Day, and Boxing Day) and social get-togethers (New Year's Eve) with high emotional intensity involving people close to the analyst. As such, the separation is often characterized as *a concentrate of Oedipus complex and primal scene*, with smouldering *feelings of exclusion rather than abandonment*.

What I want to highlight here is that *all this recurs, and the Unconscious already knows it*. It sometimes seems exactly as if the Unconscious *thinks of it* first and more than the conscious Ego, which is crisscrossed and tossed about by unexpected emotional storms whose meaning it does not recognize.

It should be said that, in most cases, *the conscious and institutionalized recurrence* is also a fact welcomed by individuals and communities, because in its positive forms (traditions, periodic celebrations, historical re-enactments) it confirms the existence and the persistence of the Self – whether individual or collective – and of the object, regardless of the nature of what is being celebrated. If it is happy, it generates joy and pride; if it is painful, at least the shared commemoration generates comfort.

We know something of this also through our institutional rituals. The whole life of our Association is marked by recurrences: the dates fixed for our scientific meetings (starting from the Wednesday ritual at Freud's house), useful certainly for planning in advance, but also for providing us with solid certainties and even with a suitable container for all our collegial ambivalences (I should not write it here, but the last-minute announcement of a speaker's absence, resulting in the cancellation of the evening's scientific event, resounds like a joyous "all free", an *ite, missa est* with its corresponding *deo gratias!*, except for the feeling, in the long run, of missing the social gathering). The congresses, the administrative meetings, even the brutal local or national elections, despite their painful turmoil, all constitute a structuring recurrence, which confirms the group Self and, consequently, the professional Self of the members.

The most individual private recurrence, on the other hand, is *the birthday*, which periodically celebrates *the intrinsic value of the birth of the subject*. The significance of this recurrence is recognized by those closest to us, and suitably confirms healthy and necessary narcissistic foundations.

Finally, we note that *while in repetition the subjective time is mostly evened out, the time of the recurrence is a rhythmic time*, which seems to preserve at least part of the sense of things changing, even in the intense perception of the experience in action.

"If Winter comes, can Spring be far behind?" sang the poet Percy Bysshe Shelley, in his famous *Ode to the western wind* (1820).

For analysts, it remains a fascinating fact that in many cases the internal pathway of the recurrence is entirely underground, complex, and ultimately spectacular, since the director organizing it remains wholly unconscious for much of its execution.

For a long time during his analysis, my patient A made a series of whirlwind existential passages, which he experienced consciously as unprecedented. After several failed relationships, which were entirely repetitive and aimed solely at narcissistic confirmations, he got married and had a daughter. Six years later, he went through a turbulent separation, got together with another woman for a couple of years, and then went back to his wife who became pregnant again. "How strange…(he says, amazed, in the session)…it is only now, here with you, that I realize that the boy soon to be born (they already found out the sex) will have a nine-year-old sister, the exact same age difference between my sister and me."

Rediscovery

What is rediscovered/retrieved forms part of a generally healthy area of the experience of re-encountering objects or situations, and this area should not be considered in the same way as true repetition.

Children do not like changing holiday destination. They usually love rediscovering the same places, the same people, and the same things, after some time has passed.

Fort-Da, the game played by little Ernst Wolfgang Halberstadt, Freud's grandson born to his beloved Sophie (and, for the record, the only other Freud, after Anna, to become an analyst [Prengler, 2001]), is one of the classic scenes of psychoanalysis. The little boy delights in making the cotton reel disappear under the sofa (*fort* = "gone") and then reappear (*da* = "there"). This scene lets us glimpse a side of repetition that is at least partially healthy and necessary. It is the side we have all experienced playing peek-a-boo with our very young children. Staging our or their disappearance, in a rudimental and instinctive way, by hiding from sight and then reappearing with expressions of joyful amazement and reconquest, happily confirming the persistence of the object and of the subject even after a separation. In short, a training for life. And it is a game that little children adore.

The experience of rediscovery marks the resuming of contact with mental contents and with parts of the Self which had been known and then distanced or lost, and which the Ego is able – sometimes under unexpected circumstances – to reach again, thanks to a preserved or rediscovered functional mobility. The rediscovery is a marvellous sign of tendency towards psychic health, even though it can sometimes be very painful.

The reintegrative processes, so often hampered by the integration anxieties described by Gaddini (1980), are the admirable product of a great deal of analytical work and, less frequently in my opinion, of the universal experience of living.

Finally, we can say that in rediscovery the subjective experience of time is profoundly different from the two conditions described previously: it is a *time that is respectful of distance, loss, and absence*.

Therefore, the subjective experience of time in these three mental occurrences is different: *in pathological repetition, time is usually flattened out; in pathological recurrence, time is rhythmic; and in rediscovery/retrieval, time is respectful of distance, loss, and absence*.

Fundamentally, we recognise and respect the profoundly cyclic rhythm of the setting, with its seasons and separations.

And we welcome – sometimes with traces of Winnicottian-style *celebration* – the surprises of rediscovery, facilitated by the partial suspension of control and secondary logic.

In the intimacy of experiential contact with the patient's lived experience, the analyst "dollies" back and forth – to use a cinematic metaphor – alternately among the various subjective dimensions of the other, with the addition of certain specific abilities he has acquired.

I believe that, thanks to the intergenerational experience of a century of analytic sessions, many analysts today experience as profoundly natural and unsurprising the continuity between present and past, between inside and outside the session, between the stories of the family and of the individual. I also believe that analysts are able to partially submerge themselves in a subjective *zeitlos* (timeless) dimension, while still retaining their sense of time in a split-off part of the working Ego (Sterba, 1934). They know, for example, when the session will end or whether it is taking place shortly before a significant separation, or even near the anniversary of an important event for the patient, "forgotten" by the conscious Ego but not by the Unconscious, and so on.

I will attempt to describe how the analyst, at the best of times, operates on the confines between repetitive circularity and a sense of the profound continuity of time and events, a continuity that is loaded with meaning.

"Non-confusional consubstantiality"

I believe that many analysts today can go beyond theoretical hypotheses and *experientially glimpse the child, the adolescent and the adult within the patient, and perhaps even the child or adolescent (or both) within the adult*. In other words, they can experience a feeling of *complex intergenerational continuity* (Kaes, 1993; Losso, 2000, 2003; Faimberg, 1998, 2005), and rediscover in the "now", as in the "then", the repeated implosion and scars of previous traumas. They can also tolerate well enough in the session the symbolic equivalence and alternation of primary and secondary processes, as part of the way of being human, in a continual coming and going between what is logical and what is *only* psychological.

In the unforgettable *One Hundred Years of Solitude* (1967), with resigned and perceptive foresight, Gabriel García Márquez depicts the same recurring existential and character traits in people of the same family, spanning ten decades.

On screen, in *2001 – A Space Odyssey* (1968), Stanley Kubrick represents the recurring cycle from the foetus to the adult to the old man, and then back to the foetus again, in an eternal return of the *monolith*.

This monolith is *timeless*, but not at all motionless: within it, the evolutionary polymorphism of the human being is represented through an incessant transformation, but also through a meaningful continuity of identity (it is always the same individual that changes over time). What is more, this polymorphism is recurrent (evolutionary cycles repeat in circles).

In the spectator, this generates a gradually expanding ability to recognize the same individual even if that individual's morphology changes, and – correspondingly – to accept the idea of an individual that changes while preserving both "substance" and identity: continuity and recurrence allow the object to be recognized, despite its incessant transformation.

Likewise, in my opinion, in many present-day analysts an internal representational area has formed and developed which is capable of containing an object in constant movement towards a *zeitlos* (timeless) state. This is an internal space in which repetition is contained as the re-presentation of that which is unrepresented or unresolved in forms which are apparently different, distinct and unconnected, but whose *consubstantiality* the analyst may conceive (or at least postulate), through rediscovery.

The concept of consubstantiality is, in fact, the central theme of this brief note. It *differentiates the analytic associative combination of different things (fluctuating between analogous, similar and corresponding) from the degeneration of confusion.*

I am aware that this term is unusual in psychoanalytic literature, and that it could induce some suspicion having been common in Catholicism for centuries, where it described the symbolic equivalence between the body of Christ and the sacred host.

It is probably a reminiscence of precisely this religious tradition that has led some Latin psychoanalysts to use this term, even if in a lay sense[1].

Nacht and Viderman (1960) spoke about *consubstantial union* as a movement towards limitless fusion, in which subject and object melt into a single undifferentiated unity.

Bouvet (1956) had also spoken of the intimate link which appears in the transference relationship between analyst and patient, using the expression *consubstantial union*.

But I cite these authors here only to show that the term was used in the past in some psychoanalytic scripts, albeit rarely and in a slightly different sense than the way I use it.

Much more significantly for me, Fornari (1980) wrote that there are consubstantial signs that present the same substance of the content of the signifying and the signified, emotional signs comparable to the amulet in primitive religions. Even the earliest and most elementary utterances of sounds, which precede words, are used by the infant as transitional objects, consubstantial to the voice of the mother, in the sense that, like that sound, they are used by the baby to keep himself company in the absence of the mother.

This brings us exactly to the area I am exploring here.

The term *consubstantiality* differentiates the analytic *associative combination* of things which are different (fluctuating between what is *analogous*, *similar*, and *corresponding*), which is an essential pre-requisite for deep understanding and creative mental activity, from the *confusion* of things which are different (but appear to be the same, because of their perceptive and representational similarity), which is, by contrast, a pathological phenomenon[2].

It is interesting to note how the experience of consubstantiality is compatible with preserving a subjective sense of time, albeit partially modified, suspended, slowed down etc., whereas confusion tends to nullify it completely.

We are dealing here with the distinction between equivalence and symbolic equation.

The concept of *consubstantiality* is close to that of *equivalence*, but with an additional element of "*experiential truth*" which goes a little beyond the signifying field of semiosis. It is rather like what happens with dreams: even though there is no reality, a sense of experiential truth is often added to the semantic representation (Bolognini, 2008a).

Finally, I underline the *difference between an experience of the Self and a semiotic decoding by the Ego.*

Some authors have concerned themselves with the two sides – the creative and the pathological – of this mental sphere. For example, Ignacio Blanco (1975, 1988) with his concepts of *class* and *isomorphism*, or Fornari Fornari (1976, 1979, 1981) with that of *koinema*. However, most of the contributions, including the ones from these two important Italian authors, have focused mainly on the analysis of possible confusions in conscious life as a result of unconscious equivalences or equations.

As Hanna Segal noted, when concrete thinking prevails symbols cannot be understood as such (that would be a real symbolic equivalence), but they are instead totally experienced (and consequently misunderstood) as what they present concretely (symbolic equation).

Segal (1957, 1994) demonstrated that the capacity to symbolize is basically connected with the capacity to separate, so that symbolic equation ends up prevailing in the paranoid-schizoid position.

What I would like to examine here, on the opposite side, is the more advanced and more creative aspect of the perception and psychic utility of *non-confusional consubstantiality* as a resource for the analyst. It could be considered a sort of auxiliary dimension fostered by practical clinical experience (rather similar to Theodor Reik's [1948] famous *third ear*), which enables the analyst to expand the meaning in analysis of what is heard and done in the session.

The analyst develops, over the years, a greater ability to alternate between a reparative and a sublimating attitude that is proper of the depressive position and a capacity to partially identify with (or *empathically perceive*, in my words) the patient's paranoid-schizoid position.

This allows the analyst to experience different levels of symbolization and concreteness (i.e. of symbolic equivalence vs. symbolic equation), which correspond to different levels of the patient's mental functioning.

César Botella and Sara Botella (2001) described this attitude of the analyst, when he is available to share the patient's analytical regression functionally, as *regredience*.

In agreement with them, I am interested in the functional advantage of a temporary and regulated regression to the lived experience of *consubstantiality in timelessness*, as happens in play, with the positive contribution of illusion (Winnicott, 1971; Milner, 1955), in artistic work through *regression at the service of the Ego* (Kris, 1952; Gombrich, 1957) and, in certain cases, in dreams (Andrade de Azevedo, 1994; Bolognini, 1999, 2005) as regards the potentially creative and transformative aspects.

· Confluence and consubstantiality

The sufficiently expert analyst often feels a *natural continuity* between a number of elements: the patient's conscious narration in the *alibi et nunc* (there – or elsewhere – and now: his current relationship with objects outside the session); his unconscious reference to the relationship with the analyst (*hic et nunc*, here and now in the sessions); the mnemic trace of the *alibi et tunc* (there and then) – which is at times a little faded – in his previous narrations of childhood relations with parents or care-givers; the patient's style (so recurrent that it often becomes repetitive, automatic, perhaps even procedural) in possible relations *with all those objects which* present themselves in external reality in equivalent conditions; and, finally, the profound reality of his relations with the object in the *absolute oneiric timelessness*, which *is* and which repeats itself, unless and until further transformative developments occur.

I remember experiencing this continuity, culturally and cognitively, at the start of my analytic career, like many of my colleagues, I should imagine. At the beginning of our training, we knew that psychoanalysis seeks and establishes connections between past and present, between the world outside and inside the session, between relations with the analyst and those with other figures through shifts, projections, and condensations in the mental and relational fields; and we prepared ourselves, sometimes in a rather planned and scholastic manner, to receive the various forms, seeing things from different observation points.

Basic teachings (such as: if the patient speaks of the present, we should think of the past; if he speaks of the past, we think of the present) were handed down to us by the classic authors. Our personal experience of analysis gradually familiarized us with a certain free circulation over and beyond the categories of secondary logic.

But in all honesty, I recall that a deliberate, methodical investigative attitude prevailed over free and spontaneous associative fluidity. Over the years, I came to realise that my inner functioning had progressively changed to what I would call *a sense of "transference confluence and consubstantiality"*.

Put simply, I mean that over time and with practice, it becomes quite natural not only to theorize, but to genuinely feel, imagine, think, and portray oneself so that there cannot be great discontinuity between what the patient feels towards external objects, towards the analyst-object, towards some aspects of his remote *basic-object*, and what he will go on to feel towards future interlocutors of a certain type, *as in the past, as now here, as now outside here, as every time that….* As the object relation that lives within him and in which he lives in the depths of his self EXISTS in any case, imprinted within him, alive and ready to reproduce itself indefinitely.

Incidentally, reflecting on the intergenerational equivalence that is intrinsic to supervision (where the supervisor functions as a more expert parental figure, providing support and assistance to the young analyst, who in turn has a parental function towards the patient), I wonder if it is no accident that this way of seeing things seems to kick in more easily at a certain age – around the time we become grandparents, in an internal sense, of course, rather than concretely for the official records.

The intergenerational prospective, at that time of life, becomes broader and more profound, enabling the analyst to identify with the intensity and potential drama of the subjective *hic et nunc* of the younger or the very young, without losing sight of the complexity of the field, the number of figures alternating on the scene, the natural cycle of the generations and the intrinsic sense of repeating configurations and developments.

And so it happens that we savour again with recurrent continuity many of our passages of identity and experience, in considering our children and grandchildren, in a cyclical retrieval of the Self and its never-ending story, just like the monolith in Kubrick's film.

Of course, despite the *wide-ranging* functional prerogatives I attribute ideally (and, I realize, in a somewhat idealizing way) to contemporary analysts, the truth remains that some of us have in a sense specialized by privileging the technical and conceptual spheres of a particular time dimension among the many that exist.

There are those who work with greater conviction in the archaeological sphere, carefully reconstructing and reconnecting elements of the present to the past to give a new meaning to the present. Others, by contrast, tend to position themselves like *instant reporters*, focusing above all on what is going on now, with a feeling that only the shared present reality can be truly transformed; there are others who would withdraw from time to solemnly promulgate formulae etched in stone (e.g. certain followers of Lacan who have a tendency, at times, to hyper-idealize the style of their maestro), in order to render things absolutely timeless and dialogue directly with the fantasy; and there are many others who tackle repetitions and transference retrieval from a number of different observation points, each in his own way, we might say.

The clinical material that follows illustrates how these various temporal dimensions can become entangled in a complex way.

A session with Olympia

Olympia is a young woman of 32 with a pleasant appearance and a lively intelligence. She has been in analysis for just over two years on a four sessions per week basis. In the session immediately preceding the one I will report, she told me, with considerable pain and embarrassment, about an unpleasant episode that had occurred the previous evening. She had been driving with her husband to dinner at a friend's house when she realized she would have to meet, among others, an acquaintance of hers with whom she had always felt a kind of rivalry and who was now expecting a baby.

Olympia is highly committed to her profession, investing a great deal of time and energy in her career. Overall, she comes across more as a "girl" than an adult woman, a "partner" more than a wife.

She also preserves – not entirely consciously – her inner status of only child (which she in fact is). She no longer lives with her parents, but they live nearby and she keeps in touch regularly, while outwardly displaying a certain impatience with them.

In many ways, her life *as part of a couple* still seems to show traces of narcissism (her partner can be seen as her integrating *double* and, at other levels, as a mirror-like twin confirmation of her Self [Kohut, 1971]; this enables her to face with a greater sense of solidity the initial phases of effective separation from her parents, upon whom she is actually still very dependent).

She has always firmly declared that she has, for now, no plans or desire to become a mother (and pooh-poohs the idea when it is insinuated).

And I take her at her word, because she still seems to me to be at an earlier stage. In fact, at this moment in time, I imagine her as one of those daughters who, if they themselves had a child, would entrust the child's upbringing to their own parents, delegating real parenthood to the grandparents, and concerning themselves above all, as their true basic interest, with pursuing their professional careers.

Nevertheless, for some time now, it has been possible to perceive in her some profound developmental changes of a complex, conflictual nature. Recently, she and her husband got a puppy. True, the puppy stays at her parents' house while she is at work, but I can attest (being somewhat of an expert on the subject…) to the fact that towards this little dog she is showing a good, authentic relational flair.

As they drew up outside their friend's house, Olympia made a kind of hysterical scene, refusing to get out of the car, weeping and staring off into space. On her part, this reaction was unintentional and came despite a sense of guilt and shame. She and her husband remained locked in this neurotic impasse for several minutes until she persuaded him to take her home, without providing him with any explanation for her behaviour.

Disconcerted and furious, her husband then joined the dinner without her, diplomatically justifying her absence with an excuse.

At the end of the session, almost through gritted teeth, Olympia had admitted to having a narcissistic problem of rivalry with her pregnant acquaintance.

In the subsequent session, Olympia reported a dream. She was photographing some whales, first from the top of a rock, then directly immersed in the water. In front of the other whales, there was a *campidoglio* [Capitol] – she immediately corrects herself: *capodoglio* [sperm whale] – which was friendly and not scary. This whale was smiling, it had teeth.

While this detail is still fresh in her mind, I point out that she said *campidoglio* instead of *capodoglio*, and that the *Campidoglio* is the hill in Rome where the Mayor of the capital lives and works.

The patient's father is a senior civil servant, with whom she has an Oedipal relationship, which is intense and preferential, but somewhat ambivalent. This is something we have already noted in analysis and the patient immediately grasps the significance of her slip of the tongue.

She then smoothly associates *the whales* with pregnant women, and we comment on her pointing out that the whales had teeth, including the *capodoglio/Campidoglio*. First, she talks about a *vegetarian shark*, then she recognizes without too much resistance that the whales in her dream all seem rather ambivalent as regards their aggressiveness, and a chuckle escapes her.

She pauses briefly.

In a tone which is suddenly sombre and serious, she says that there is "only one historic photograph" of her mother when she was pregnant.

Then she adds: "If I were ever to have a child, I would never leave him with my mother …she doesn't even treat my dog well when I leave it with her …".

I say: "Let's stop here for a moment... (a short pause; I repeat her words back to her, articulating slowly so as to savour them and reconsider them together) *If I were ever to have a child* ...: here is *only one historic photograph* (a flash!) of her pregnant" (a short pause to share the time to ponder it, then I continue). "The *first – and so far the only one* – since you have been here." (another pause, to break off and create an inner space for subsequent thoughts). "I believe that *we are photographing the whale*".

I feel as if I am *in the water* with the patient, whereas I had previously been observing her *from the top of a rock*.

Who is pregnant in this scene?

Olympia, in her and our fantasy, and in her future potential? Her acquaintance-rival whom she avoided the other evening? Olympia's mother in that photograph from many years ago? The analyst as a maternal equivalent, within whom in the session Olympia grows little by little, evolves and carries out her twisting and turning associations? All those who allow others into their inner space and enable them to grow?

There is, however, a dissonant non-idyllic note in this scene which sticks in my mind, and I decide to bring it up.

ANALYST: "What about the whales with teeth?"
PATIENT (with a kind of sarcastic snicker through clenched teeth): "Eh-eh!!!..." (Olympia has a strange idiosyncratic way of speaking through clenched teeth: she clenches her teeth *not to say things*, as if she were trying to stop herself, then ends up saying them, but through clenched teeth, in a continual inner compromise between expressing things and holding them back. From her voice, I imagine her eyes sparkling, somewhere between the fear of daring and the excitement of being aggressive) "I was in the water, no longer at a distance on the rocks ...I was not scared, but I was so close...".
ANALYST (hearing the negation in the word not): "Perhaps you were a little afraid; but you were still close. And you saw the whales for the first time close up, from within their environment."

I think that *being on the rocks*, in a safe place *from above*, also connects with a particular defensive identification with her father (*hard as a rock*), and with a certain way of treating things *from the top down* which is typical of him, and which I also see in Olympia when she imitates him unconsciously.

The watery *amnios* in which she is diving, in analysis, seems to signify now her initial approach to the maternal world, and consequently a different contact with her own Self.

I don't share these thoughts with her, though, as they are very general.

Up to this point, technically, all I have done is follow her, pointing out what she has said and exploring what was manifest.

Through the narration of the dream and its reverberation within me, I experienced an intense emotion at the appearance – on the analytic scene – of these enormous, primitive animals, equivalent to her pregnant mother, capable of provoking positive and negative feelings of great intensity.

At this point, I decide to create a further connection, still using the elements the patient has brought to the session, aimed at giving representative form (by means of a metaphoric equivalence which seems in that moment to be effective and freely circulating) to the lived experience which I feel has established itself in the *here and now*: "your dog also has teeth, but you like to keep it close to you".

This is the cue for a childhood Self-object (her dog) to enter the scene, one that she often mentions fondly and finds reassuring. Perhaps it carries with it an unconscious intention on my part to reassure (and, in that case, it is an expression of my defence against the overwhelming emotion and closeness of the encounter with *the pregnant mother*, whom I have also become through the transference)? Or, on the other hand, am I opportunely highlighting the feeling we share that this important moment can be liveable notwithstanding the complexity of ambivalence (the dog also has sizeable teeth)?

Whatever the effective liveability may be, this passage of images and emotions between the two of us in the session remains a pretty extraordinary moment, one that is neither normal nor obvious. It is exactly like seeing whales at close quarters. A powerful and unforgettable experience, according to those who have had the privilege of seeing them in real life.

I think that a very similar effect is to be had when one emerges from the protective narcissistic prospective to recognize the object, with all the admiring impact that entails, and with a subsequent, inevitable ambivalent reaction towards the object.

My clinical reflections turn to ponder this last aspect, that of conflictual ambivalence.

I wonder: who *has teeth*, in that dream scene? Who has teeth in the scene of the session?

Olympia, who is getting closer to me, or I myself, who am getting closer to her, in an analytic relational medium where the physical laws of other environments no longer apply, and *one floats* a great deal more?

Olympia with her old unsettled scores with her mother (who found herself pregnant at a very early age, against her own will and that of her parents, and who significantly celebrated her unwanted pregnancy with a single, paltry photograph), or Olympia who is resentful of her father, the *vegetarian shark* who prevents her (and himself) from reaching their incestuous goal?

Her father, *Campidoglio-capodoglio*/mayor-head of the *family/national capital*, who stands ambivalently between her and her *pregnant mother/other whales*, or rather between her and her potential motherhood?

Or perhaps even her *puppy dog*/herself as a child, who is growing (as she herself is growing here in analysis) but whom she likes to be with all the same and who is not dangerous even though he gnaws on everything to *sharpen his teeth*?

Or Olympia-the bloodthirsty rival, who could tear to pieces her acquaintance (as well as myself as an adult capable of containing her and helping her grow) to rob her of not *one*, but *the* pregnancy?

I feel there is some continuity in all this, though we must gradually bring into focus the predominant accumulations of meaning.

I also think about the moment when her eighteen-year-old mother had to tell her parents, through clenched teeth, that she was pregnant, and her fear of their *teeth*, of their bites [*morso* in Italian] and of her own inner remorse [*ri-morso*]. I also think about how Olympia has to avoid doing as her mother did, and perhaps has to make up, through her own career, for all that she deprived her mother of by being born.

There is a consubstantiality between the whales, the pregnant mothers, the analysts who creatively contain their patients *until term*, the patients who begin to imagine their own inner space after they had conflictually admired and envied those of others.

There is consubstantiality between the teeth of a playful puppy, between those of Eve/Olympia whose desire is to bite into the scandalous apple of adulthood, and the explorative-separative teeth of the analyst who, by cutting, separating and differentiating, interprets and distinguishes between what is vital and what is deadly in the mental life of his patients.

At times, we analysts use this metaphorical consubstantiality in a natural way, deliberately talking about whales in order to talk about mothers, about a certain historic mother of the past, or a potential mother-to-be in the patient's future, or to talk of motherhood in general, when we feel that the patient is able to follow us, that the patient shares the flow of the Preconscious, and *sees* – in those rare, privileged moments – the profound connections, the equivalence between things which are apparently so different and distant from one another, things which have come to us from their dreams, associations and fantasies.

We often have to wait years before the patient has made enough progress to share with us the creative dimension of *non-confusional consubstantiality*, in which the working Ego can immerge itself in the Preconscious and periodically re-emerge, in the necessary comings and goings between the many symbolic equivalences and the different ways of mental functioning.

We analysts also progress, with experience and reflection, in this complex activity, and I believe that young candidates in supervision, who sometimes ask me if at that particular point in the session it would have been useful, or indeed possible, to provide the patient directly with an interpretation of the transference, will find their own original answers – alongside the technical ones available in the literature, which are important nonetheless – in their own personal equation, connected to their deeper internal evolution.

And this is also true for Olympia. Aside from the analytic episode I have reported, I still cannot determine with any degree of certainty her present ability to contact and explore her inner world, or the true extent of the ongoing changes in her object relations.

We will see, over the next few months.

Yet, a feeling is taking shape that Olympia has made her way *into the water*.

It is not quite clear whether she fell in or chose to dive in, but by this stage we are swimming in the analytic field and great, eternal, archaic fantasies from the past and perhaps from the future are coming towards us. As in her early childhood, as in the history of previous generations of her family, as in the generations which could descend from Olympia, if everything goes well enough, as in the generations of analysts that could descend from me and from my colleagues, as happens...*every time that...* someone contains someone else with sufficient creativity and a genuine desire to make them live and grow, as happened to us.

What becomes crucial, then, is not the repetition in itself but *how* one repeats and *with whom*, in order to escape the diabolical vortex of compulsion and reach, sooner or later, the longed-for shore of benign, shared rediscovery/re-experiencing, which is at the same time the necessary prerequisite and the precious fruit of psychoanalytic *durcharbeiten* (working through).

Notes

1 Of the Anglo-Saxon authors, Loewald (1979) was the only one who oddly – but intentionally – used Latin terms in his contribution: "insofar as the oedipal objectum is consubstantial, as it were, with the preoedipal identificatum – is the same body as that with whom the identificatory bond existed and still persists – the preoedipal bond is violated. (I use the Latin expressions objectum and identificatum for what I hope will be greater clarity of meaning)" (p. 765).

2 In physics, *analogy* (from the Greek *anà-loghìa* = proportion) signifies the relationship of affinity between two different phenomena whose sizes are connected to identical proportional equations. In biology, it indicates a morphological or functional similarity between two organs, different one from the other in their structure or development. In both cases, the similarity is given by the proportional relationships. In mathematics, *correspondence* refers to the relationship between two or more elements of two different classes, which relate to each other either spatially or functionally. Still in mathematics, *similarity* refers to figures which have the same shape, but different dimensions. In psychological terms, analogy refers to a more marked evocative function than similarity: that is, it provokes a more direct mental connection with what can be associated to what is perceiveda and less confusion between the two.

BIBLIOGRAPHY

Adler, A. (1911), "Beitrag zur Lehre von Widerstand". In *Zentralblatt der Psychoanalyse*, 1, 215 N.
Alvarez, A. (2017), "The role of emotion in thinking: Technical issues arising from the problem of deficits in the internal object". Contribution at the meeting "*Interpretare: parola, voce, transform/azione. Percorsi della "talking cure"*, Centro Milanese di Psicoanalisi, 9 giugno 2018.
Andrade De Azevedo, A.M. (1994), "Validación del proceso clínico psicoanalítico. El papel de los sueños". In *International Journal of Psychoanalysis*, 10, pp. 191–205.
Atwood, G., Stolorow, R. (1984), "*Structures of Subjectivity*". The Analytic Press, Hillsadale (NJ).
Bach, S. (2016), "*Chimeras and Other Writings. Selected Papers by Sheldon Bach*". International Psychoanalytic Books (IPB), New York.
Baranger, M., Baranger, W. (1969), "Problemas del campo psicoanalítico" *[Problems of the Analytic Field]*. Kargieman, Buenos Aires.
Bertolucci, A. (1929), "Assenza". In *Sirio*. Alessandro Minardi, Parma.
Bibring, E. (1943), "The conception of the repetition compulsion". In *Psychoanalytic Quarterly*, 12, pp. 486–519.
Bion, W.R. (1962), "Learning from experience". In *Seven Servants*. Aronson 1977, New York.
Bion, W.R. (1971), "Attention and interpretation". In *Seven Servants*. Aronson 1977, New York.
Bleger, J. (1967), "*Simbiosis y ambiguedad., estudio psicoanalitico*". Buenos Aires: Editorial Paidòs.
Bollas, C. (1987), "*The Shadow of the Object. Psychoanalysis of the Unthought Known*". New York: Columbia University Press.

Bolognini, S. (1991), "Gelosie progressive" (Progressive jealousy). In *Gli Argonauti*, 13, 48, pp. 45–56.

Bolognini, S. (1997), "Empatia e patologie gravi" (Empathy and Serious Pathologies). In Correale, A., Rinaldi, L. (a cura di), *Quale psicoanalisi per le psicosi?* (*Which kind of Psychoanalysis for the Psychosis?*) Raffaello Cortina, Milano.

Bolognini, S. (1999): "Lavoro del sogno, lavoro con il sogno", In Bolognini, S., Boringhieri, B. (Ed.), *Il sogno cent'anni dopo*.

Bolognini, S. (2002), "Psychoanalytic Empathy". London: Free Association Books (2004).

Bolognini, S. (2004), "La complexité de l'empathie psychanalytique: Une exploration théorique et clinique". In *Revue Française de Psychanalyse*, 3, pp. 877–896.

Bolognini, S. (2005), "Il bicchiere mezzo vuoto o mezzo pieno: lavoro del sogno ed elaborazione onirica". In *Psicoanalisi e metodo*, 5, pp. 79–100.

Bolognini, S. (2008a), "Secret Passages. The Theory and Technique of Interpsychic Relations". Routledge, (2011).

Bolognini, S. (2008b), "Real wolves and fake wolves. Alternating between repression and splitting in complex clinical cases". In Bokanowsky, T., Lewkowicz, S. (Eds.), *Splitting of the Ego in the Process of Defense*. IPA Publications, Karnac, London.

Bolognini, S. (2010a), "Passaggi segreti verso l'inconscio. Stili e tecniche di esplorazione"(Secret Passages to the Unconscious. Styles and Techniques for Explorations". In *Rivista di Psicoanalisi*, 3, pp. 599–613.

Bolognini, S. (2010b), "Empatia, atmosfera, rappresentazione. Nota clinica su una prima seduta". (Empathy, Atmosphere, Representation. A clinical note about a first session) In *Psicoterapia Psicoanalitica*, xvii, 2, pp. 9–18.

Bolognini, S. (2010c), "Contratransferencia y atmosfera: Una sesion con Antonia". In *Docta*, 6, pp. 74–78.

Bolognini, S. (2013a), "Die institutionelle und die innere Familie des Analytikers". In *Forum der Psychoanalyse*, 29, 3, pp. 357–372.

Bolognini, S. (2013b), "In spite of my Ego. Problem solving and the unconscious". In Kay O'Neill, M., Akhtar, S. (a cura di), *On Freud's "The Unconscious"*. Karnac, London.

Bolognini, S. (2014a), "Interpsychique, intersubjectif, interpersonnel: Etats et passages". In *Revue Psychosomatique*, 45, pp. 143–161.

Bolognini, S. (2014b), "Lo interpsíquico: Estado normal, patología y las diferencias con lo interpersonal e intersubjetivo". In *Revista de Psicoanálisis de la Asociacion Psicoanalitica de Madrid*, 71, pp. 3–23.

Bolognini, S. (2014c), "Il femminicidio. Le radici profonde della violenza maschile contro le donne". *Conferenza a Il lettino e la piazza*, Biblioteca Sala Borsa, Bologna, 8 marzo.

Bolognini, S. (2014d), "Inauditum/Unerhoert!!!… Gewissen, Bewusstsein, Integration. Die Analyse als posttraumatische Erfahrung". In *Unherhoert – Vom Hoeren un Verstehen*, edited by I. Bozetti, I. Focke, I. Hahn. Fachbuch Klett-Cotta, Stuttgart.

Bolognini, S. (2015a), "In between sameness and otherness. The analyst's words in interpsychic dialogue". In Joyce, A. (edited by), *Donald W. Winnicott and the History of the Present*. Karnac, London, pp. 17–30.

Bolognini, S. (2015b), "Vinculos y intimidad". In *Revista Peruana de Psicoanalisis*, 16, pp. 11–20.

Bolognini, S. (2016a), "The interpsychic dimension in the psychoanalytic interpretation". In *Psychoanalytic Inquiry*, 36, pp. 1–10.

Bolognini, S. (2016b), "Plaisir, maîtrise et légitimation narcissique, les points cardinaux de la perversion". In *Le Coq Heron. Voix de la psychanalyse italienne, aujourd'hui*. Erés, Paris.

Bolognini, S. (2016c), "Elementi di tecnica tra Sé e non-Sé" (Elements of Technique between Self and Not-Self). In *Rivista di Psicoanalisi*, lxii, 1, pp. 5–26.

Bolognini, S. (2017a), "Conviction, persuasion, suggestion". In Abella, A., Déjussel, G. (a cura di), *Conviction, Suggestion, Seduction*. Presses Universitaires de France, Paris, pp. 51–62.

Bolognini, S. (2017b), "Zwischen Gleichsein und Anderssein. Die Worte des Analytikers im interpsychischen Dialog". In *Forum der Psychoanalyse*, 33, pp. 385–399.

Bolognini, S. (2018), "Incanti e disincanti nella formazione e nell'uso delle teorie psicoanalitiche sulla realtà psichica" (Enchantments and disenchantments in the formation and use of psychoanalytic theories about psychic reality). In *Rivista di Psicoanalisi* (The Italian Psychoanalytic Annual), 3, pp. 533–548.

Bonfiglio, B. (2018), "*Simbiosi, fusionalità e costruzione della soggettività. Parlando di clinica*". FrancoAngeli, Milano.

Bonfiglio, B. (2019), "Il difficile viaggio alla scoperta della fusionalità". Relazione al convegno *Fusionalità. Storia del concetto e sviluppi attuali*, Roma, 23–24 marzo.

Botella, C., Botella, S. (2001), "*La figurabilité psychique*". Delachaux et Niestlé, Lausanne/Paris.

Bouvet, M. (1956), "La clinica psicoanalitica. La relazione oggettuale". Tr. it. in *A che punto è la psicoanalisi*. Gherardo Casini, Roma 1969, pp. 35–86.

Busch, F. (2014), "*Creating a Psychoanalytic Mind*". London: Routledge.

Busch, F. (2019), "*The Analyst's Reveries. Explorations in Bion's Enigmatic Concept*". Routledge, London-New York.

Campanile, A. (1974), "Paganini non ripete". In *Asparagi e immortalità dell'anima*. Rizzoli, Milano.

De Bono, E. (1970), "*Lateral Thinking. Creativity Step by Step*". Harper, New York.

De Moncheaux, C. (1978), "Dreaming and the organizing function of the ego". In *International Journal of Psychoanalysis*, 59, pp. 443–453.

Duncker, K. (1945), "On problem solving". *Psychological Monographs*, 58 (5, Whole No. 270).

Faimberg, H. (1998), "Transgenerationnel-Intergenerationnel". In De Mijolla, A. (Ed.), *Dictionnaire International de la Psychanalyse*. Dunod, Paris.

Faimberg, H. (2005), "*The Telescoping of Generations. Listening to the Narcissistic Links between Generations*". Routledge, London-New York.

Faimberg, H., Kaes, R., Enriquez, M., Baranes, J.J. (1993), "*Transmission de la vie psychique entre générations*". Dunod, Paris.

Falci, A. (2017), "Le implicazioni dei 'sistemi mirror' e della 'simulazione incarnata' nelle teorie della mente e nelle attuali concezioni teoriche e cliniche delle psicoanalisi contempranee". In Busato Barbaglio, C., Meterangelis, G., Pirrongelli, C., Solano, L. (a cura di), *Anticipare il futuro. La psicoanalisi oggi*. FrancoAngeli, Milano, pp. 239–266.

Ferro, A. (1994), "Del campo e dei suoi eventi". In *Quaderni di Psicoterapia infantile*, 30.

Ferro, A. (1995), "Lo sviluppo del concetto di campo in Europa". Relazione alla "Giornata in onore di Willy Baranger", Buenos Aires.

Ferro, A. (1998), "Il sogno della veglia. Teoria e clinica". In *Rivista di Psicoanalisi*, 44, pp. 117–128.

Ferro, A. (2001), "*Seeds of Illness and Seeds of Recovery. The Genesis of Suffering and the Role of Psychoanalysis*". Routledge/New Library, London.

Filippini, S., Ponsi, M. (1992), "Sul concetto di preconscio". In *Rivista di Psicoanalisi*, 38, 3, pp. 639–685.

Fliess, R. (1942), "The metapsychology of the analyst". In *Psychoanalytic Quarterly*, 11, pp. 211–227.

Fonda, P. (2000), "La fusionalità e i rapporti oggettuali". In *Rivista di Psicoanalisi*, 3, pp. 429–449.

Fonda, P. (2019), "La fusionalità. Uno dei meccanismi elementari dello psichismo umano". Relazione al convegno *Fusionalità. Storia del concetto e sviluppi attuali*, Roma, 23–24 marzo.

Fornari, F. (1976), "*Simbolo e codice*". Feltrinelli, Milano.

Fornari, F. (1979), "*Cinema e icona*". il Saggiatore, Milano.

Fornari, F. (1980), "*I fondamenti di una teoria psicoanalitica del linguaggio*". Boringhieri, Torino.

Fornari, F. (1981), "*Il codice vivente*". Boringhieri, Torino.

Fosshage, J. (1997), "The organizing functions of dream mentation". In *Contemporary Psychoanalysis*, 33, pp. 434–458.

Freud, S. (1905), "Three Essays on the Theory of Sexuality". S.E., 7.

Freud, S. (1914), "Remembering, repeating and working-through". S.E., 12.

Freud, S. (1915a), "Mourning and Melancholia". S.E., 14.
Freud, S. (1915b), "The Unconscious". S.E., 14.
Freud, S. (1920), "Beyond the Pleasure Principle". S.E., 18.
Freud, S. (1938), "An Out-Line of Psychoa-Analysis". S.E., 23.
Gabbard, G.O., Wilkinson, S.M. (1994), *Management of Countertransference with Borderline Patients*. American Psychiatric Press, Washington, DC.
Gaddini, E. (1980), "Note sul problema mente-corpo". In *Scritti*. Raffaello Cortina, Milano 1989.
Gaddini, E. (1982), "Acting out in the psychoanalytic session". In *International Journal of Psychoanalysis*, 63, pp. 57–64.
Gallese, V., ET AL. (2003), "The roots of empathy: The shared manifold hypothesis and the neural basis of intersubjectivity". In *Psychopathology*, 36, 4, pp. 171–180.
García Márquez, G. (1967), *Cent'anni di solitudine*. Tr. it. Feltrinelli, Milano 1968.
Garma, A. (1970), *Nuovi studi sul sogno*. Astrolabio Ubaldini, Roma 1974.
Godfriend-Haber, J., Haber, M. (2002), "L'expérience agie partagée". In *Revue française de psychanalyse*, 66, 5, pp. 1417–1460.
Goldberg, A. (1994), "Farewell to the objective analyst". In *International Journal of Psychoanalysis*, 75, pp. 21–30.
Gombrich, E. (1957), *Arte e illusione. Studio sulla psicologia della rappresentazione pittorica*. Tr. it. Einaudi, Torino 1965.
Green, A. (1974), "Surface analysis, deep analysis. The role of the preconscious in psychoanalytical technique". In *International Review of Psychoanalysis*, 1, pp. 415–423.
Green, A. (1993), *"The Work of the Negative"*. London: Free Association Books (1999).
Green, A. (1998), "The primordial mind and the work of the negative". In *International Journal of Psychoanalysis*, 79, pp. 649–666.
Green, A. (2000), "The intrapsychic and intersubjective in psychoanalysis". In *Psychoanalytic Quarterly*, 69, pp. 1–39.
Greenberg, J. (2001), "The analyst's participation. A new look". In *Journal of the American Psychoanalytic Association*, 49, 2, pp. 359–381.
Greenberg, J. (2012), "Alterità e analisi dell'azione". Letto al Centro Psicoanalitico di Bologna il 19-4-2012.
Greenberg, R., Katz, H., Schwartz, W., Pearlman, C. (1992), "A research-based reconsideration of the psychoanalytic theory of dreaming". In *Journal of the American Psychoanalytic Association*, 40, pp. 531–550.
Greenberg, R., Pearlman, C. (1993), "An integrated approach to dream theory. Contributions from sleep research and clinical practice". In Moffitt, A., Kramer, M., Hoffmann, R. (a cura di), *Suny Series in Dream Studies. The Functions of Dreaming*. State University of New York Press, Albany (NY), pp. 363–380.

Greenson, R. (1954), "Il suono mmm". Tr. it. in *Esplorazioni psicoanalitiche*. Bollati Boringhieri, Torino 1999.

Grinberg, L., ET AL. (1967), "Funzione del sognare e classificazione clinica dei sogni nel processo analitico". In *Revista de Psicoanalisis*, 24.

Grinberg, L., Grinberg, R. (1976), *Identidad y cambio*. Ediciones Paidós Iberica, Barcelona.

Guss Teicholz, J. (1999), *Kohut, Loewald and the Postmoderns. A Comparative Study of Self and Relationship*. The Analytic Press, Hillsdale (nj), pp. 182–189.

Hartmann, H. (1964), *Essays on Ego Psychology: Selected Problems in Psychoanalytic Theory*. International Universities Press, New York.

Heimann, P. (1950), "On countertransference". *International Journal of Psychoanalysis*, 31, 81–84.

Heimann, P. (1956), "Dynamic of transference interpretations". *International Journal of Psychoanalysis*, 37, 303–310.

Herrigel, E. (1948), *Lo Zen e il tiro con l'arco*. Tr. it. Adelphi, Milano 1999.

Jacobs, T.H. (1986), "On countertransference enactment". In *Journal of the American Psychoanalytic Association*, 34, pp. 289–307.

Jacobson, E. (1964), "*The Self and the Object World*". New York: International University Press.

Kaes, R. (1993), *Le groupe et le sujet du groupe*. Dunod, Paris.

Kaes, R., Faimberg, H., Enriquez, M., Baranes, J.J. (1993), *Transmission de la vie psychique entre générations*. Dunod, Paris.

Kahn, L. (1914): "Le psychanalyste apathique et le patient postmoderne". Editions de l'Olivier, Penser/Rever, Paris.

Klein, M. (1955), "On identification". In "*New Directions in Psycho-Analysis*". London: Tavistock.

Klein, M. (1961), "*Narrative of a Child Analysis*". Hogarth, London.

Kohut, H. (1971), "*The Analysis of the Self*". London: Hogarth Press.

Kramer, M. (1993), "The selective mood regulatory function of dreaming: An update and revision". In *The Functions of Dreaming*. Moffitt, Albany, New York State University Press.

Kris, E. (1952), "*Psychoanalytic Explorations in Art*". New York: International University Press.

Lagache, D. (1951), "Le problème du transfert". In *Revue Française de Psychanalyse*, 16, 102.

Lagache, D. (1953), "Alcuni aspetti della traslazione". Tr. it. in Genovese, C. (a cura di), *Setting e processo analitico. Saggi sulla teoria della tecnica*. Raffaello Cortina, Milano 1988.

Laplanche, J., Pontalis, J.-B. (1967), *Enciclopedia della psicanalisi*. Tr. it. Laterza, Roma 1973.

Loewald, H. (1979), "The waning of the Oedipus complex". In *Journal of the American Psychoanalytic Association*, 27, pp. 751–775.

Lombardozzi, A. (2019), "Stati fusionali e funzioni di oggetto Sé. Configurazioni del campo analitico". Relazione al convegno *Fusionalità. Storia del concetto e sviluppi attuali*, Roma, 23–24 marzo.
Lopez, D. (1976), *Aldilà della follia, aldilà della saggezza*. Guaraldi, Rimini.
Lopez, D. (1983), *La psicoanalisi della persona*. Boringhieri, Torino.
Losso, R. (2000), *Psicoanalisi della famiglia. Percorsi teorico-clinici*. FrancoAngeli, Milano.
Losso, R. (2003), "L'intrapsichico, l'interpersonale e il transpsichico nella psicoanalisi di coppia". Relazione al Centro Psicoanalitico di Firenze, 30 gennaio.
Maeder, A. (1912), "Uber die Funktion des Traumes". In *Jahrbuch für psychoanalytische und psychopathologische Forschung*, 4, 2, pp. 692–707.
Mahler, M.S. (1968), *On Human Symbiosis and the Vicissitudes of Individuation*. International Universities Press, New York.
Mahler, M.S. (1972), "On the first three subphases of the separation-individuation process". In *International Journal of Psychoanalysis*, 53, pp. 333–338.
Matte Blanco, I. (1975), *L'inconscio come insiemi infiniti*. Tr. it. Einaudi, Torino 1981.
Matte Blanco, I. (1988), *Pensare, sentire, essere*. Tr. it. Bollati Boringhieri, Torino 1995.
Matte Blanco, I. (1975), *The unconscious as infinite sets*. London: Karnac.
Meterangelis, G. (2019), "Fusionalità e svolta relazionale". Relazione al convegno *Fusionalità. Storia del concetto e sviluppi attuali*, Roma, 23–24 marzo.
Metcalfe, J., Wiebe, D. (1987), "Intuition in insight and noninsight problem solving". In *Memory & Cognition*, 15, pp. 238–246.
Micati, L. (1993), "Quanta realtà può essere tollerata?". In *Rivista di Psicoanalisi*, 39, pp. 153–163.
Milner, M. (1955), "The role of illusion in symbol-formation". In *"New Directions in Psychoanalysis"*, London: Tavistock.
Nacht, S., Viderman, S. (1960), "The pre-object universe in the transference situation". In *International Journal of Psychoanalysis*, 41, pp. 385–388.
Negri, R. (1994), *Il neonato in terapia intensiva. Un modello neuropsicoanalitico di prevenzione*. Raffaello Cortina, Milano.
Nietzsche, F. (1882), *La gaia scienza*. Tr. it. Einaudi, Torino 2015.
Ogden, T.H. (2003), "This art of psychoanalysis. Dreaming underdreamt dreams and interrupted cries". In *International Journal of Psychoanalysis*, 85, pp. 857–878.
Osborn, A.F. (1962), "Developments in creative education". In Parnes, S.J., Harding, H.F. (a cura di), *A Source Book for Creative Thinking*. Scribners, New York, pp. 19–29.
Pallier, L. (1990), "Fusionalità". In Neri, C., Pallier, L., Petacchi, G., Soavi, G.C., Tagliacozzo, R. (a cura di), *Fusionalità*. Borla, Roma.

Pazzagli, A. (2017), "La sindrome di Stendhal e la nosografia psichiatrica". In *Psicoanalisi*, 1, pp. 103–110.

Pessoa, F. (1982), "*Il libro dell'inquietudine di Bernardo Soares*". Tr. it. Feltrinelli, Milano 2013.

Pierri, M. (2018), "*Un enigma per il Dottor Freud. La sfida della telepatia*". FrancoAngeli, Milano.

Pine, F. (1990), "*Drive, Ego, Object & Self. A Synthesis for Clinical Work*". Basic Books, New York.

Prengler, A. (2001), "El ninho del carretel: Una visita a Ernst Freud". In *Fort-Da – Revista de Psicoanalisis con ninhos*, 3, aprile.

Racamier, P.C. (1992), "Il genio delle origini" *(The Genius of Origins)*. Tr. it. Raffaello Cortina, Milano 1993.

Reik, T.H. (1948), "*Listening With the Third Ear. The Inner Experience of a Psychoanalyst*". Grove Press, New York.

Rizzolatti, G., Sinigaglia, C. (2006), "*So quel che fai. Il cervello che agisce e i neuroni specchio*". Raffaello Cortina, Milano.

Rosenfeld, H. (1971), "A clinical approach to the psychoanalytic theory of the life and death instincts: An investigation into the aggressive aspects of narcissism". In *International Journal of Psychoanalysis*, 52, pp. 169–178.

Rosenfeld, H. (1987), "*Impasse and Interpretation*". Tavistock Publications, London.

Rumiati, R. (2006), "Creatività". In *Psiche. Dizionario di psicologia, psichiatria, psicoanalisi, neuroscienze*. Einaudi, Torino.

Sander L.W. (1975), "Infant and caretaking environment: Investigation and conceptualization of adaptive behaviour in a system of increasing complexity". In Anthony, E.J. (Ed.), *Explorations in Child Psychiatry*. Plenum Press, New York.

Schafer, R. (1959), "Generative empathy in the treatment situation". In *Psychoanalytic Quarterly*, 28, pp. 347–373.

Schafer, R. (1964), "The clinical analysis of affects". In *Journal of the American Psychoanalytic Association*, 12, pp. 275–299.

Schafer, R. (1983), "*The Analytic Attitude*". London: Karnac.

Segal, H. (1957), "Notes on symbol formation". In *International Journal of Psychoanalysis*, 38, pp. 391–397.

Segal, H. (1994), "Phantasy and reality". In *The Contemporary Kleinians of London*. International Universities Press, New York.

Shelley, P.B. (1820), "Ode to the west wind". In "*Prometeus Unbound. A lyrical Drama*". London: C. and J. Ollier.

Soavi, G.C. (1989), "Il mito dell'eterno ritorno e la sua importanza nella strutturazione del Sé". In *Rivista di Psicoanalisi*, 35, pp. 787–805.

Spitz, R.A. (1965), "*The First Year of Life: A Psychoanalytic Study of Normal and Deviant Development of Object Relations*". New York: International Universities Press.

Bibliography

Stahl, F. J. (1830), "Introduction". In *Die Philosophie des Rechts nach Geschichtlicher Ansicht*. Heidelberg. Pp. XXV.

Steiner, J. (1993), *"Psychic Retreats: Pathological Organizations in Psychotic, Neurotic, and Borderline Patients"*. London: Routledge.

Sterba, R. (1934), "The fate of the Ego in analytic therapy". In *International Journal of Psychoanalysis*, 15, pp. 117–126.

Tustin, F. (1981), *"Autistic States in Children"*. London: Routledge and Keagan Paul.

Yalom, I. (1970), *"The Theory and Practice of Group Psychotherapy"*. New York: Basic Books.

Van Os, J., Reininghaus, U. (2016), "Psychosis as a transdiagnostic and extended phenotype in the general population". In *World Psychiatry*, 2, pp. 118–124.

Wallas, G. (1926), *"The Art of Thought"*. Watts, London 1949.

Wertheimer, M. (1945), "Productive thinking". New York: Harper. *Il pensiero produttivo*.

Widlöcher, D. (2001), "The treatment of affects. An interdisciplinary issue". In *Psychoanalytic Quarterly*, 70, pp. 243–264.

Widlöcher, D. (2003), "La personne du psychanalyste et les processus d'empathie et de co-pensées". In *Bulletin Féderation Européenne de Psychanalyse*, 57, pp. 89–95.

Winnicott, D. (1971), *"Playing and Reality"*. London: Tavistock.

Wisdom, J.O. (1967), "Testing an interpretation within a session". In *International Journal of Psychoanalysis*, 48, pp. 44–52.

INDEX

acclimatization, 11
adolescent-onset psychosis, 92
Alvarez, Anne, 111
analytical journey, 11
Antonia's psychoanalytic treatment: anxieties, 40; components of idealization, 40; first consultation, 37–39; idealizing sacredness and humanization of feelings, 39; neurotic condition of unhappiness and inconclusiveness, 37; relationship between defensive Ego and Self, 41–42; relationship with grandparents, 39–40; unexpected discontinuities, 41
après-coup psychoanalytic reflection, 108
assessment, problem-solving stage, 23

Bolognese Apennine hills, 2–3
Botella, César, 135
Botella, Sara, 135
Brahmanism, 114
brainstorming, 24

Campanile, Achille, 125
central Ego, 16, 21, 26, 32–33, 34, 46, 61; *see also* Ego
central ego, 16
Chimera (Bach), 68
cinema, 2
clandestine therapeutic alliance, 65
cognitive psychology, 23

"concave" containing-receptive function, 101
confluence, 135–137
conscious Ego, 17–18, 22, 128–129, 132; *see also* Ego
conscious imitation, 26
consubstantiality, 134, 135–137
consubstantial union, 133
cooperation, 17, 33
co-pensér (co-thinking), 65
co-thinking, 72
countertransference reaction, 43, 58, 66, 111, 113
creative corporeal conjunctions, 60

De Bono, Edward, 24
defensive ego, 12
deidealizing intuition, 28–29
depersonnalisation, 64
depersonnation, 63–65, 66
dis-identification process, 115, 117
Divine Comedy/analytic competence, 102–103, 105
dream: examples of, 19; experiential dimension of, 18; functions of premeditation, 18; in phases of integration, 18

Ego, 62; central, 16, 21, 26, 32–33, 34, 46, 61; conscious, 17–18, 22, 128–129, 132; conscious Central, 60; energy expenditure and ego functioning, 29–32;

Index

functioning, 91–94; as objects for consultation, 27; working, 9, 24; *see also* Self
ego-self relationship, 96–100
empathy, 13, 72
energy expenditure and ego functioning, 29–32, 118; optimal reduction of, 32
energy savings, intra- and interpsychic, 11
envy feeling, 15
Eskimo roll technique, 126–127
everyday environments, 2

family relationships, 1
fantasmatic base camp, 1
Fornari, Fornari, 134
functional fixedness, 24, 27, 28
functional *We*, 66

Greenson, Ralph, 79
Group Psychology and the Analysis of the Ego (Freud), 65

Herrigel, Eugen, 4
Hinduism, 114

idealization of object, 77
illumination, problem-solving stage, 23
impersonal pronoun, 78–79
incubation, problem-solving stage, 23
internal relationship with object, 27
International Psychoanalytical Association (IPA), 45
interpersonal bond, 57
interpersonal concept, 54, 59, 66–69
interpersonal contact, 39
interpersonal dispositions, 43
Interpretation of Dreams (Freud), 6
interpsychic concept, 54, 59, 66–69, 68; in clinic, 69–73
interpsychic contact, 39
interpsychic sucking process, 66
interpsychic syntonization, 79–80
interpsychic tools, 74–77
intersubjective common/condominium spaces, 68
intersubjective concept, 59, 66–69; in clinic, 69–72
intimacy, 45–52; belonging and loyalty in, 55–58; as co-created and co-creating condition, 54–55; dimensions, 48; in dual relationship, 56–57; healthy, 49; libidinal bonds and, 55–58; mode of intimate interchanges, 48; in mother-baby relationship, 46; pathological intimate exchanges, 53–54; physiological fusional phase, 46; schematic representation of relational vector, 56–57; in terms of symbiosis and fusionality, 46
intrapsychic geographies, 2
introjection, 10
intuition, 22–25; connections between cognitive theories and psychoanalytic view of, 25–28; degrees and types of interiorization, 26–27; deidealizing, 28–29
invisible symbioses, 1

kaleidoscope effect, 32
knowledge of unconscious, 7–8
Kohut, Heinz, 28–29, 30

lateral thinking, 24
libido-emotional cachexia, 100

mafia clans, 2
messenger, 12–13
metaphors: for conscious interpersonal communication, 12; little guatemalan dolls, 21–22, 25; medieval, 13; "Puss in Boots" fable, 19–21; of submarine, 9
Metcalfe, Janet, 24
minimal technical tools, 74
mirroring castles, 13
mirroring neurons, 13
"Mmmmh…." sound, 79–80, 101
Mourning and Melancholia (Freud), 97

non-confusional consubstantiality, 132–135, 135
non-confusional fusionality, 79
Non-Self, 14, 59, 63, 68, 69, 74, 78

object deprivation, 111
Ode to the western wind (Shelley), 130
One Hundred Years of Solitude, 132
oneirology, 17, 19
Open Sesame! moment, 5
Others, 16

Paganini, Niccolò, 125
parent-child intrapsychic couple, 88

Index

partial introjective identifications, 25–27
partial non-confusional fusionality, 60
person, defined, 67
Piccard, Jacques, 7
Pierri, Maria, 128
placental nutrition, 100–101
Poincaré, Henri, 23
polymorphism, 133
preconscious, 6–7, 14, 16–17, 21; practicable, 11; psychic life, 11; *see also* unconscious
presubjective and preanalytic patients, 83–90; Giorgia, 84; Grazia, 84–85; Renata, 85–90
problem-solving stages, 23
professional Ego, 51
professional Self, 31, 51
projective identification, 72
psychic equivalents of vital bodily functions, 60
psychic retreats, 111
psychoanalysis, 5, 6, 91, 120; forms of identifications, 10; *Fort-Da* game, 131; patient's initial expectations of therapeutic process, 8; session with Olympia, 138–144; submarine metaphor, 9
psychoanalysts, 5, 7; analytical vision, 8; areas of competence, 8
psychoanalytic empathy, 43–44
psychoanalytic object relations theory, 28
psychoanalytic psychotherapy, 93–94; analytic encounters, 114–118; case of Alvaro, 101–106; ego-self relationship, 96–97, 96–100; episode of re-integration, 94–95; integrative levels in ego functioning, 95–96; regressive hole concept, 108–110; separation experience, 112–114; treatment of serious pathologies, 106–108
psychoanalytic theory, 9
psychosis, 91–92
psychotic disorder, 91–92

recurrences, 127–130
rediscovering, 130–132
regredience, 119, 135
regression, 11
regressive hole concept, 108–110
relational anorexia, 100
relational co-habitability, 62

relational quality, 61–62; inter- and intra-psychic aspects, 62–63
repetition, 121–127
representation to internal worlds, 42
river-stone masonry, 3
Rosenfeld, Herbert, 116

Secret Passages, 71
Segal, Hanna, 134
Self, 14, 20, 33, 59, 62, 68–69, 74, 76, 78, 82; compartmentalized, simplified, and impoverished condition within, 31; day zone, 29; dissociative and substitutive processes of, 117; experiential, 61; non-confusional extension of, 63; primary anxiety and, 110–112; professional, 31; social adaptation, 118; working, 9; *see also* Ego
self-awareness, 95
separation experience in analysis, 112–114
shared co-thinking contact, 79
Spitz, René, 111
splitting/dissociation, 31
Steiner, John, 111
subject, defined, 66–67
subjective formulation, 24, 27, 28, 30
superego, 12, 50

task preparation, problem-solving stage, 23
therapeutic alliance, 80; clandestine, 101; preconscious resonant nuances, 80–82; transference relationship, 133; use of "we" in interpsychic level, 82
therapeutic process: intersubjective and interpersonal bond, 57–58; patient's initial expectations of, 8
Three Essays on the Theory of Sexuality, 60
transference, 41, 43, 76, 81, 82, 99, 101, 104, 108, 110, 112, 113, 121, 123, 126, 133, 136, 137, 141, 143
transference-countertransference dynamic, 66
transpsychic concept, 59
trial identifications, 10
Twenty Thousand Leagues under the Sea, 8
2001 – A Space Odyssey, 132

unconscious, 5–6, 21, 34–36, 84–85, 89, 97–98, 108, 119, 121, 125–127,

129–130, 132, 134–135, 141; as an area of active transformation, 18–19; cooperation, 65; forms of identifications, 10; Freudian passages, 16–17; memory, 127; parasitic clandestinity, 72; sensible, 18; *see also* preconscious
universality of experience, 77

Wallas, Graham, 23
Wertheimer, Max, 24
Wiebe, David, 24
working ego, 9
working self, 9

Zen and archery (Herrigel), 4

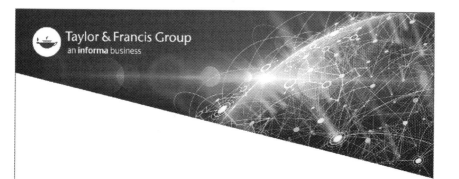

Printed in the United States
by Baker & Taylor Publisher Services